# THE HOLY SPIRIT:

## 592 Verses Examined

**Katheryn Maddox Haddad**

# Other Books by the Author

CHRISTIAN LIFE
Applied Christianity: Handbook 500 Good Works
You Can Be a Hero Alone
Worship Changes Since 1st Century + Worship 1sr Century Way
The Best of Alexander Campbell's Millennial Harbinger
Inside the Hearts of Bible Women-Reader+Audio+Leader
The Lord's Supper: 52 Readings with Prayers

BIBLE TEXTS
Revelation: A Love Letter From God
The Holy Spirit: 592 Verses Examined
Was Jesus God? (Why Evil)
365 Life-Changing Scriptures Day by Date
Love Letters of Jesus & His Bride, Ecclesia (Song of Solomon)
Christianity or Islam? The Contrast
The Road to Heaven

FUN BOOKS
Bible Puzzles, Bible Song Book, Bible Numbers

TOUCHING GOD SERIES
365 Golden Bible Thoughts: God's Heart to Yours
365 Pearls of Wisdom: God's Soul to Yours
365 Silver-Winged Prayers: Your Spirit to God's

SURVEY SERIES: EASY BIBLE WORKBOOKS
→Old Testament & New Testament Surveys
→Questions You Have Asked-Part I & II

HISTORICAL RESEARCH BIBLE
for Novel, Screenwriter, Documentary & Thesis Writers

HISTORICAL NOVELS & STORYBOOKS
Series of 8: They Met Jesus
Ongoing Series of 8: Intrepid Men of God
Mysteries of the Empire with Klaudius & Hektor
Christmas: They Rocked the Cradle that Rocked the World
Series of 8: A Child's Life of Christ
Series of 10: A Child's Bible Heroes
Series of 8: A Child's Bible Kids
Series of 10: A Child's Bible Ladies

GENEALOGY: Climb Your Family Tree w/o Falling Out
Volume I & 2: Beginner-Intermediate & Colonial-Medieval

Copyright ɢ 2014 Katheryn Maddox Haddad
**ISBN  978-1-948462-92-1**
**NORTHERN LIGHTS PUBLISHING HOUSE**

Printed in the United States

# IN PRAISE OF THE HOLY SPIRIT: 592 VERSES EXAMINED

An Excellent Read & Training. An excellent Christian book on the Holy Spirit. Very thorough and interesting. I never read any book that explained it so well, since I read the Bible itself. Very educational.

ScienTechie

I really enjoyed reading this book.

Christine George.

Just started it because of a large amount of reading but it is a great help.

Roland

# Table of Contents

IN PRAISE OF THE HOLY SPIRIT: .......................................... iii
How This Book Was Researched & Written ........................... vi

1. Relationship With
Old-Testament-Times Believers In General ............................ 1
2. Relationship With
Old Testament Prophets ................................................ 8
3. Relationship In
The Transition From Old To New Testament ........................ 14
4. Relationship With
 New Testament Apostles ............................................ 19
5. Relationship With
New-Testament-Times Believers In General – I
(Before New Testament Written) .................................... 27
6. Inch-By-Inch Study
 Of Tongues ......................................................... 30
7. Relationship With
New-Testament-Times Believers In General II
(Before New Testament Written) .................................... 38
8. Inch-By-Inch Study
 Of Acts 2 Prophecies ............................................... 43

9. Attributes Of The Holy Spirit – I ................................ 48
10. Attributes Of The Holy Spirit – II ............................... 55

11. Relationship With
Believers
(After The New Testament Was Written-I) ........................ 60
12. Relationship With
Believers
(After The New Testament Was Written-II) ....................... 70
13. Relationship With
The Whole World ~ I ................................................. 78

14. Relationship With
The Whole World ~ II......................................86

15. Relationship With
God The Father ........................................93
16. Relationship With
God The Son.............................................100

Thank You ................................................109
Buy Your Next Book Now ........................110

About The Author .....................................111
Connect With The Author.........................112

Get A Free Book........................................112
Join My Dream Team ...............................112

ALL VERSES WITH THE WORD "SPIRIT"...........113

# How This Book Was Researched & Written

There are numerous books on the Holy Spirit, but they are based on only a few Bible verses. This study was not done to prove the author's or anyone else's pet assessment of the Holy Spirit. The study was made with the desire to forget all pre-conceived notions and opinions, and discover only God's opinion.

The Bible has **592 verses saying Holy Spirit and God's Spirit**. This is the only book of its kind to cover all verses. All other books take a few ideas about the Holy Spirit and elaborate on them.

To make sense out of **all 592 verses**, they were categorized according to what you see in the table of contents in this book ~ the types of people affected by the Holy Spirit.

Within each category, are sub-categories, usually based on how the Holy Spirit connected with each person, and how each person reacted.

The same subcategory terms will sometimes appear in each category of the people the Holy Spirit affected. At first, those little words may seem to have no particular significance. But as you progressed through them, you will see that even little words like "within" and "upon," and "full" sometimes had big significance. All those word studies prepare you for the even more dynamic later chapters in the book.

Read through these chapters, not to prove what you already believe, but with an open mind and heart that perhaps you don't believe in enough things the Holy Spirit does, or you believe in more things than the scriptures actually teach.

Let us be careful that we do not go beyond what is written (I Corinthians 4:6). Now, let us gear up for all things God's Holy Spirit does, and get ready to be amazed.

# 1. Relationship with Old-Testament-Times Believers in General

First, what does the word spirit mean? Everyone has a spirit. We say when someone dies that their spirit left their body. So, our spirit is what gives us life. Therefore, God's Spirit is his life force. Remember before God created the heavens and the earth. His Spirit hovered over the waters, ready to bring everything into existence.

God the Father willed it, God the Son Spoke it, and God the Spirit gave it existence.

## WITHIN

*Isaiah 63:11-12; I Corinthians 10:1-4*

There is only one scripture regarding Old Testament believers, in general, referring to the Holy Spirit being within people. Isaiah 63:11-12 says that, when Moses and the Jews escaping their slavery in Egypt reached the Red Sea, God "remembered Moses and his people" and put his Spirit "**within** them" as they walked through the sea on dry land.

It must have taken all the courage they could muster to step foot on that seabed. Trembling, they must have looked from side to side at the waters, wondering if they would hold long enough for them to get to the other side. Trembling, wondering, and maybe thinking it was all a dream. But it was reality. An amazing reality.

When we have the Holy Spirit within us, he can stop the floods of animosity or danger around us while we pass through. There is a parallel thought about God's Spirit being within people in the New Testament. When we drink, that substance goes within us. I Corinthians 10:1-4 recalls how the Jews drank the same spiritual drink from the spiritual Rock, which was Christ. Elsewhere Jesus said he was the water of life.

1

# UPON – Physically

*Judges 3:10-11; Judges 6:34; 7:12, 21; Judges 11:1,29,33; Judges 14:5-6;
Judges 14:19a; Judges 15:14-15
Zechariah 4:6-9*

In the books of Judges, God's Spirit came or fell upon four different men in different decades, but all under the same circumstance. The first occurrence is Judge Othniel. "The Spirit of the Lord **came upon** Othniel, " and he judged Israel and went to war where he conquered their enemies (Judges 3:10-11).

Later, "the Spirit of the Lord **came upon** Gideon," he blew his trumpet and the entire enemy army, as numerous as the sands on a seashore, fled. (See Judges 6:34; 7:12 & 21.)

Further along in the book of Judges, "the Spirit of the Lord **came upon** Jephthah" who led his army to the Ammonites and Midianites where they defeated twenty Midianite kings. (See Judges 11:1, 29, 33.)

Interestingly, the Spirit of God came upon Samson, and he single-handedly did a lot of killing. When he was confronted by a lion, "the Spirit of the Lord **came mightily upon** him, " and he tore the lion apart. Then he proceeded to Ashkelon where "the Spirit of the Lord **came upon him mightily**," and he killed thirty men. (See Judges 14:6 and 19.) When three thousand Jews went to him and said he was just making their enemy madder, he let them tie him up with ropes so they could deliver him to the Philistines. That didn't last long. When they got him close to a Philistine city, "the Spirit of the Lord **came mightily upon** him, " and he broke the ropes binding him as easily as we would break strings that had been burned. Then he proceeded to kill a thousand men with a donkey's jawbone. (See Judges 15:11-15.)

But there was an instance of spiritual power and might in the Old Testament that caused people to have the will to use their physical skills. God told the prophet, Zechariah, to tell Zerubbabel, the Persian-selected governor of Palestine, "not by **might** nor by **power**, but by my Spirit" the foundation of the temple had been laid.

When considering the superhuman strength the Spirit gave Samson, we can understand the superhuman spiritual strength God's Spirit can give in the spiritual realm, the realm where willpower makes all the difference in the world, sometimes without our realizing just how superhuman it is.

## UPON – Mentally & Spiritually

*Numbers 11:25; Numbers 24:1-2; 31:8; Judges 3:10-11; I Samuel 10:1-7; I Samuel 18:10-12; I Samuel 19:18-24;*
*I Chronicles 12:14-18; II Chronicles 15:1, 8; II Chronicles 20:14-15.*

What the Spirit of God did physically to those judges, he also did mentally and spiritually. In understanding how powerful the Spirit can be in the material world, it helps us understand how powerful the Spirit can make someone in the spiritual world.

The book of I Samuel reveals some interesting things about the workings of the Spirit on King Saul. Samuel anointed Saul the first Jewish king. Then he told him to go to where the enemy Philistine garrison was, and there he would meet a group of prophets prophesying. "Then the Spirit of the Lord will **come upon** you, and you will prophesy with them and be turned into another man." What did he prophesy? We don't know, but perhaps it was "You cannot win."

He told Saul that it would happen to him periodically. In other words, that special gift of prophecy did not stay with Saul all the time but did sporadically. (See I Samuel 10:1, 5-7.)

But much later, after King Saul became jealous of the giant killer, David escaped his now-jealous king. So King Saul sent soldiers to capture David. But, when they came near to where David was, they met Samuel and some others all prophesying. Then, much to everyone's surprise, "the Spirit of God **came upon** the messengers of Saul, and they also prophesied. When the captains returned to Saul to tell him what happened, he sent them out again. This happened three times, and all three times, the Spirit of God **came upon** them, and they prophesied.

So, now Saul took things into his own hands, and he personally went out to capture (or kill) David. When he got as far as Samuel and his prophets, the same thing happened to Saul: "The Spirit of God was upon him also, and he went on and prophesied." He did not pursue David further. Was the prophecy that he would lose? You can read all about this in I Samuel 19:20-24.

Interestingly, then, God made people who were full of hatred (such as Saul's toward David) to prophesy. There is something similar to this in the New Testament. Philippians 1:15-18 speaks of preachers full of envy and strife who were proclaiming Christ out of selfish ambition. Paul said they didn't need to be stopped because at least they were preaching Christ, and he would rejoice in their message, though not in the men themselves.

Back in the Old Testament, when some of the strongest men in Saul's army defected to David, the Spirit of the Lord **came upon** the chief of the thirty strongest men, and he declared that God was with David and he would prevail (I Chronicles 12:1-18). The word prophecy isn't in this passage, but that is what Amasai was doing.

Centuries later, during the reign of King Asa, "the Spirit of God **came upon**" Azariah who went to the king to tell him God would be with him as long as he was faithful. Thereupon, King Asa destroyed all the idols in the land and repaired the altar of the Lord in the temple (II Chronicles 15:1-8).

Years after that when Jehoshaphat was king, a vast army of Moabites and Ammonites from Edom headed to Jerusalem to destroy it. "The Spirit of the Lord **came upon**" a little-known Levite named Jahaziel. He went to the king and declared something we sometimes quote even today: "Do not be afraid or discouraged because of this army. For the battle is not yours, but God's."

Jumping to the Christian era, we know the church has always had its enemies. At first, it was the pagans with their false gods, lasting in some parts of Europe up to the Middle Ages. Then it was the Muslims against whom misdirected Christians led crusades. Then it was infighting within the church. For awhile, it was Buddhism, Hinduism, the New Age movement, and atheism that precipitated by wars in the Far East. Now some major enemies of the church are Muslims.

Remember, this chapter is how God's Spirit came upon ordinary people and worked through them. What advice did Paul give young Timothy? "God did not give us a spirit of timidity, but a spirit of power, of love, and of self-discipline."

Today, we must bravely stand before our enemies, not flinching, refusing to give in to them, standing firm and not deserting our post. We must fight. But fight with words, the Sword of the Spirit, and with Love that conquers all. And never, ever, ever back down.

### Saved or Not?

The word "prophecy" comes from the Hebrew word, *naba* meaning to abundantly utter or pour out. A marvelous example of "pouring out" is Jeremiah who was made the laughing stock of Jerusalem, and lost all his friends for predicting Jerusalem's fall. He wanted to just quit prophesying altogether. But then he wrote this:

> *But if I say, "I will not mention him or speak anymore in his name,"*
> *His word is in my heart like a fire,*
> *A fire shut up in my bones.*
> *I am weary of holding it in;*
> *Indeed, I cannot!*
> Jeremiah 20:9

So now, we come to another misconception of what God's Spirit does. Many believe that, once God's Spirit comes upon someone, he stays permanently. That is not true, as was seen above in the case of Saul and his soldiers.

An extension of this belief is that, if the Holy Spirit comes upon someone, it proves they just got saved. We shall now consider Balaam.

Numbers 24:1-2 said Balaam was a sorcerer for the king of Moab. He was probably what we would call a priest. Kings in the first few millenniums of the earth usually surrounded themselves with priestly advisors to keep them in good standing with the gods. Numbers 23 and 24 explain how Balaam prophesied in favor of the Israelites on more than one occasion. But did it last?

Revelation 2:14 recalls that Balaam taught people should eat food sacrificed to idols and commit sexual immorality. The apostles said in II Peter 2:15 that Christians who fall away are following the way of Balaam. So, we know Balaam only prophesied as God told him to temporarily. Then what happened to him in addition to him reverting to his old teachings? The Israelites killed him (Numbers 31:8).

## FILLED/FULL

*Exodus 28:3; Exodus 31:3-5; Exodus 35:30-35; Deuteronomy 34:9*

There are two instances among ordinary people in the Old Testament of people being filled with the Holy Spirit. They both were given mental powers.

In Exodus 28:3, it explains that God gave wisdom to men to make garments for the priests and high priest. Three chapters later in Exodus 31:1-5, the Lord said of Bezaleel, "I have **filled** him with the Spirit of God" to have skill in all kinds of crafts in wood and precious metals. It was Bazaleel who led in the construction of the tabernacle and all the furnishings in it.

Later, Joshua in Deuteronomy 34:9, was "**filled** with the spirit of wisdom" so he could lead the Israelites after Moses died, and take them into their Promised Land.

So, it is not always the prophet who God's Holy Spirit helps. God gives talents to many people. We may not be filled with the particular talents we want or many talents, but we all have some talents to some degree. Skills in craftsmanship were important long ago, and they still can be important. We can help people in our neighborhood, our congregation, our city, or even people in other nations with our craftsmanship talents. We do not need to be highly intelligent or even reach the stature of a great prophet for God to use us. God needs everyone, and now.

# 2. Relationship with Old Testament Prophets

## Came or Fell UPON

*I Samuel 16:13; II Chronicles 24:20-21; Ezekiel 2:2; 3:2;
Ezekiel 3:24-27*

### SPIRITUAL

When the Spirit of God **came upon** Zechariah, a priest, he stood on a platform above the people and declared that, since they had forsaken the Lord, the Lord had forsaken them. He had hoped they would develop fear in their heart because God had given up on them (II Chronicles 24:20-21). Indeed, in tat case, they should have feared!

We often talk about being saved, and we automatically think about going to heaven. But what are we being saved from? When we're saved while swimming, we don't think of getting better at it, but being saved from drowning. When someone is saved during a mountain climb, it doesn't mean he was saved to reach the top but saved from falling.

What fire are we being snatched from so we can be saved from it? What darkness? What pain? What tears? What are we being saved from?

Perhaps we should bring up hell more often. Many people are converted because they fear hell. They don't fall deeply in love with God until they mature in the faith more. They are grateful to God, but the kind of love that makes them want to be with God more than they fear hell comes later. We need to bring out people's fears more.

These people did not fear the priest of God, for they decided to stone Zechariah, kill the messenger. But the Holy Spirit was upon him, and he had to speak the message of God.

(The prophet who wrote our "book" of Zechariah in the

Bible was a different Zechariah.)

Long before either of these Zechariahs, God's Spirit came upon David when Samuel anointed him king (I Samuel 16:13). But he did not come upon David for a specific message. "The Spirit of the Lord **came upon** David from that day forward." In fact, Peter, on the Day of Pentecost called David a prophet (Acts 2:29-30). That is how we know all the psalms that David wrote were inspired by God.

Further, David made numerous prophecies about Jesus, his descendant, that he would be betrayed, afflicted, deserted, estranged, slandered, mocked, hated, tried, pierced, be buried, then come back to life from the grave. His prophecies are found in Psalms 8, 18, 21, 22, 23, 34 35, 37, 38, 40, 41, 42, 44, 55, 69, 88, 102, 19, 116, 118 and others.

## BOTH PHYSICAL & SPIRITUAL

Some people speak of being "slain in the Spirit" and falling down. But notice how Ezekiel responded. "The Spirit entered me when he spoke to me, and set me **upon** my feet" then gave him a message to pass on to God's rebellious, impudent and stubborn people (Ezekiel 2:25). God warned him that the people may or may not listen to him, but he was to go and speak anyway.

It happened again in Ezekiel 3:24-27. This time "The Spirit entered me and set me **upon** my feet," same as before. Next, God told him he was to enter his house, be bound with ropes so he could not leave. Further, he would not be able to speak until God gave him a message to give the people.

Notice what was similar in both cases. The Holy Spirit did not make Ezekiel fall down onto the floor. The Spirit made him stand up. Never, in the entire Bible, did the Holy Spirit ever make someone fall down.

## Went/Lifted/Took/Brought UP

*II Kings 2:9-11; II Kings 2:16; Ezekiel 3:12-15; Ezekiel 8:3a;*

*Ezekiel 11:1-2; Ezekiel 11:24; Ezekiel 37:1; Ezekiel 43:1-5*

## LITERAL MOVEMENT TO HEAVEN

Let's look at Elijah. II Kings 2:16 says that Elijah's students thought the Spirit of the Lord had **taken** him **up** to some mountain or down into a valley. What had actually happened is that the Spirit of the Lord had taken him all the way up to heaven (verses 9-11).

So, when the Christian dies, surely it is God's Holy Spirit who takes us from this life to the next in glory. What comfort. What gladness. We are never left alone.

## MOVEMENT BY VISION TO HOLY PLACE

All of the instances noted below happened to Ezekiel, the one God's Spirit stood up onto his feet, as stated above. Chapter 3, verses 12 and 13 explains that, when Ezekiel was **lifted up**, he went in a vision to heaven.

In 8:3; 11:1-2,24; and 43:1-5, Ezekiel, while in Babylon (today's Iraq), he was **lifted up** by the Spirit and brought by visions of God to the temple in far-off Jerusalem. It had to have been a vision because the temple in Jerusalem had been destroyed. Then God's Spirit **lifted** him **up** again and returned him to Babylon.

One time, the Spirit of the Lord **brought** him to a valley full of bones (Ezekiel 37:1). This too, of course, was a vision. If you read the whole account, you will see that Ezekiel watched flesh return to the bones and life returned to the bodies ~ all in his very symbolic vision. Even today this vision can be a comfort because there can be a congregation about to die, but God puts new life into it and it grows again. The same with individuals falling away.

A later vision ~ Ezekiel's final vision ~ was when God's Spirit **brought** him to the east gate of Jerusalem. Remember, Jerusalem had been destroyed, and this was only a vision. Then the Spirit **lifted** him **up** and brought him to the inner court of the temple. This vision was reassurance that both the holy city of

Jerusalem and the temple would be rebuilt someday.

What comfort to the Jews far from their homeland. As nations fall today, we can take comfort that perhaps some day in another generation it can rise again by returning to God.

# CARRIED/TAKEN

*I Kings 18:12; II Peter 1:20-21; Micah 3:8*

## LITERAL MOVEMENT TO ANOTHER PLACE

Elijah told Obadiah to tell the king where he was hiding. But Obadiah objected, saying that the king might punish him for giving false information. He said, "...the Spirit of the Lord will **carry** you to a place I do not know" (I Kings 18:12).

This does not say whether it involved walking to another location or suddenly appearing in another location. The important thing is that movement occurred.

## SPIRITUAL MOVEMENT OF THE MIND

Peter, in the New Testament, explained that the prophets were **carried along** by the Spirit to write the Scriptures (II Peter 1:20-21). Some translations say they were **moved**, but it comes from the same Hebrew term.

We must never forget when we read those words on the pages of our Bible that a real person was carried along by the Spirit, was inspired by the Spirit to write those words down so they could be preserved from one generation to another for thousands of generations yet unborn. How blessed we are.

# SPEAK/SPOKE/PROPHECY

*Deuteronomy 34:9-10; I Samuel 16:13 (Acts 2:29-30); I Samuel 19:20; II Samuel 23:1-2; II Kings 2:5, 15, 17; Nehemiah 9:30; Zechariah 7:11-*

*12; Matthew 22:43; Acts 1:16; 2:29-28;*
*I Peter 1:10-12; II Peter 1:20-21*

When the Spirit moved a prophet, he spoke the words of the Lord. Here is a list of all such statements in the writings of each of the prophets in the Old Testament.

David (Psalms) "the Lord spoke by me"
Isaiah – visions and "the Lord said"
Jeremiah – "the word of the Lord came unto" and "the Lord said"
Ezekiel – visions and "the word of the Lord came unto"
Daniel – visions
Hosea – "the word of the Lord came unto" and "the Lord said"
Joel – "the word of the Lord came to"
Amos – visions and "Thus says the Lord" and "hear the word"
Obadiah – vision
Jonah – "the word of the Lord came unto"
Micah – "the word of the Lord came to" and "the Lord said"
Nahum – "the burden of the vision"
Habakkuk – "the burden he saw"
Zephaniah – "the word of the Lord came unto"
Haggai – "the word of the Lord came unto"
Zechariah – "came the word of the Lord unto"
Malachi – "the burden of the word of the Lord"

A special note here about David. II Samuel 23:1-2 says God spoke by him, and Peter referred to David in several places in Acts 1 and 2 as the prophet "through whom the Holy Spirit spoke." If the Holy Spirit spoke through David, he did so through all the prophets.

## FILLED/FULL

The prophet, Micah, said he was **full** of power by the Spirit of the Lord to declare his message (Micah 3:8). When something is full, it can easily spill over. When poured out, it comes rushing out.

The word "prophecy" literally means to pour out. Jeremiah 20:9 explains this phenomenon that prophets experienced. I quoted it in chapter one, but it is so dynamic, so heart-stirring, here it is again:

> *But if I say, "I will not mention him or speak anymore in his name,"*
> *His word is in my heart like a fire,*
> *A fire shut up in my bones.*
> *I am weary of holding it in;*
> *Indeed, I cannot!*

# 3. Relationship in the Transition From Old to New Testament

## RESTED ON

*Numbers 11:25; II Kings 2:15; Isaiah 11:1-2; Zechariah 6:5, 8;
Acts 2:1-4, 14; I Peter 1:1-2; 4:14;*

Can you imagine having something on your heart so strong that you have to talk about it? Today we are compelled to talk about new babies, new jobs, new cars, monumental birthdays and so on. We can hardly hold it back. We want to share the news with everyone. But it does not compare with the compulsion the prophets felt to pour out what God told them to say.

This is a very exciting chapter. We will only discuss one way the Holy Spirit influenced someone, and that way is that he **rested on** certain people. This means the Holy Spirit came and stayed while. The Hebrew word, *nuach,* means to lie down, be at rest, stay. Some very fascinating things are revealed when studying the little phrase, **rested on.**

The prophets must have all felt compelled to write those words, just as Jeremiah expressed so aptly above.

### Moses

Numbers 11:25 says the Lord came down in a cloud and took of the Spirit that was upon Moses and placed it upon the seventy elders. "And it happened, when the Spirit **rested on** them, that they prophesied."

Later, Moses himself passed it on to Joshua: "Now Joshua the son of Nun was full of the Spirit of wisdom, for Moses had laid his hands on him" (Deuteronomy 34:9).

Do we have any evidence that the seventy elders or Joshua were able to pass the Spirit on to others? Only Moses had that power.

What was special about Moses? To the serious Bible student, it is evident. Moses introduced the Law to the Israelite nation, what we call the Law of Moses. His representing the Old Testament era of the Law was also evident at Jesus' transfiguration (Luke 9:29-31).

## Elijah

II Kings 2:15 explains that the Spirit in Elijah **rested on** Elisha. Elijah first appears in I Kings 17:1 and was the first of a long line of significant prophets from then on in the Old Testament.

Do we have any evidence that Elisha was able to pass the Spirit on to others? Only Elijah had that power.

What was special about Elijah? Most Bible students say he introduced the era of prophets in the Old Testament. In fact, he represented the prophets at Jesus' transfiguration (Luke 9:29-31).

## Apostles

Now read Acts 2:1-4 carefully. "When the Day of Pentecost had fully come [a different day from when the 120 were gathered together in chapter 1], they were all with one accord in one place. And suddenly there came a sound from heaven, as of a rushing mighty wind, and it filled the whole house where they were sitting. Then there appeared to them divided tongues, as of fire, and one **sat [rested]** upon each of them. And they were filled with the Holy Spirit and began to speak with other tongues as the Spirit gave them utterance."

The same Greek word translated "sat" in this passage ~ *kathizo* ~ is also translated **rested** in many other scriptures.

Who were the people who received the Holy Spirit in this manner? The NIV is clearest. In verse 7, the people out on the street referred to them as men from Galilee. Peter said in verse 15 that these men were not drunk. In verse 27, the audience asked Peter and the other apostles what to do to be saved. So, they were all men and all apostles.

15

Were the apostles able to pass on the Spirit to others? Yes, they were, just like Moses and Elijah were. Acts 8:18 says it was through the laying on of the apostles' hands that the Holy Spirit was given. The apostle Paul said in Romans 1:11 that he longed to see the Christians in Rome so he could impart spiritual gifts to them.

Were those people able to pass the Spirit on to someone else? There is no evidence they were ever able to do that; otherwise, why did they have to send for an apostle to do it?

What was special about the apostles? They introduced the Christian era.

## Christians

Peter wrote to Christians scattered throughout today's Turkey ~ Pontus, Galatia, Cappadocia, Asia and Bithynia, all Roman provinces in that area between the Middle East and Europe. In I Peter 2:14, he said, "…the Spirit of glory and of God **rests upon** you." Not everyone he wrote to in that vast country (much larger than Greece and Italy combined, and close to the same size as most of the Middle East) could perform miracles. So, we see Peter was specifically talking about something God's Spirit does for Christians in general. All one has to do is to go back to Peter's first sermon in Acts 2:38 to see that he is referring to the forgiveness of their sins, their salvation.

## The World

Zechariah predicted in 6:5 and 8 that it was on people moving north of Jerusalem that God's Spirit would come to **rest**. What is north of Jerusalem? A lot of the Middle East is, a lot of the Far East is, and all of Europe is.

## Rested and Remained On

## JESUS

At last, we come to the culmination of all this, for it was only on Jesus that God's Spirit rested and remained on.

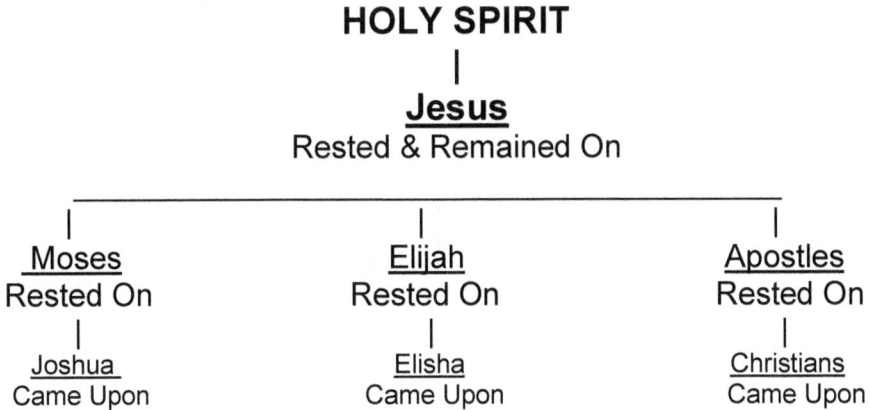

## HOLY SPIRIT
|
### Jesus
Rested & Remained On

| | | |
|---|---|---|
| | | |
| Moses | Elijah | Apostles |
| Rested On | Rested On | Rested On |
| | | |
| Joshua | Elisha | Christians |
| Came Upon | Came Upon | Came Upon |

Isaiah 11:1-2 predicted it: "There shall come forth a Rod from the stem of Jesse, and a Branch shall grow out of his roots. The Spirit of the Lord shall **rest upon** him, the Spirit of wisdom and understanding, the Spirit of counsel and might, the Spirit of knowledge and of the fear of the Lord."

Where was the Branch of David to live? Isaiah 9:1 said it would be in Galilee. Matthew 4:13-14 says that's where Jesus lived. In fact, the people at Jesus' triumphant entry into Jerusalem called him that predicted Son of David (Matthew 21:7-9).

Now, look at John 1:33 and 34. " 'I did not know him, but he who sent me to baptize with water said to me, Upon whom you see the Spirit descending and **remaining on** him, this is he who baptizes with the Holy Spirit. And I have seen and testified that this is the Son of God.' "

Who introduced the Christian era, according to Hebrews 8:13 and 16? Jesus did. But he had a special power Moses and Elijah did not have. He passed on the part of God's Sprit to his apostles (John 20:19-24), and also he gave them the power to pass it on to others.

So, you see how exciting a word study of the Holy Spirit can

17

be.  What's next?  Let's find out.

# 4. Relationship With New Testament Apostles

We will now repeat some of the ways the Holy Spirit came to prophets in the past as discussed in chapters one and two, but this time it will be how he affected the apostles.

## POWER

*Acts 1:8; Romans 15:18-19; I Corinthians 2:4; I Thessalonians 1:5*

All scriptures relating the Holy Spirit to power refers to miracles. The word in Greek is *dunamis*, sometimes also translated "mighty works" or "miracles". In Acts 1:8, Jesus promised his apostles they would receive power when the Holy Spirit came upon them. Paul recalled in Romans 15:18-19 that the Gentiles obeyed because he had performed "mighty signs and wonders, by the **power** of the Spirit of God". Paul told the Corinthians that his sermons were demonstrated by the Spirit and **power.** Finally, he told the church in Thessalonica that the gospel came to them both in word and **power** in the Holy Spirit.

People of the first century had to have some proof that the words just spoken to them were actually from God. The signs, wonders, and miracles provided that evidence. Today, we do not need those signs of God's power because those words have been written down in a book with built-in proofs of its own that it is of divine origin ~ archaeological, historical, and extant manuscript evidence.

## FILLED/FULL

*Acts 9:15-17; Acts 11:22-24; Acts 13:8-11*

In Acts 9:15-17, Paul was **filled** by the Holy Spirit with a desire to carry Jesus' name before the Gentiles and their kings, as well as the Jews. In Acts 11:22-24, Barnabas was **full** of the Holy Spirit and faith. See here how God's Spirit helped them desire to seek and teach the lost.

But also, the Holy Spirit **filled** Paul and gave him the ability to strike someone blind because he was deceiving the people. This was an indirect way of spreading the gospel by stopping those who tried to stop its progress.

Again, whenever the Spirit filled someone, that person had a strong compulsion to fulfill what the Spirit urged them to do. Of course, they could have fought the Spirit and disobeyed, but Paul and Barnabas did not. They listened and acted.

## Went/Lifted/Took/Brought/Caught/ Carried/Taken

*II Corinthians 12:1-2; Revelation 17:3; Revelation 21:9-10*

## MOVEMENT BY VISION TO A SATANIC OR HOLY PLACE

With the power of God's Spirit, Paul was **caught up** to the third heaven, though he could not tell if it were a vision or literal. (See II Corinthians 12:1-2).

In the last book of the Bible, the apostle John was **carried** into a desert where he saw paganism riding on the back of the beast of paganism (Revelation 17:3). Later, he was **carried** to a great and high mountain where he saw the New Jerusalem with its pearly gates, crystal walls, and gemstone foundation stones (Revelation 21:10).

Never in any of the 592 scriptures did the Spirit take or bring someone down.

## IN
*Romans 9:1; Revelation 1:10; Revelation 4:2*

The Holy Spirit was **in** Paul, proving he was telling the truth (Romans 9:1). John was **in** the Spirit on the Lord's Day when he heard Jesus call to him (Revelation 1:10). Later, while **in** the Spirit, John beheld the throne of God in heaven.

When God's Spirit was in them, something happened. They spoke, they heard, they acted. It was not a passive thing.

## SPECIAL PROMISES

*Matthew 10:1-4; Matthew 10:1, 19-20; John 7:38-39; John 20:19-22;*
*Acts 1:2 – 5; Acts 2:1-4*

Jesus gave his apostles special powers to perform miracles ~ a special gift of the Holy Spirit. Also, the Spirit of God spoke through them (Matthew 10:14 and John 7:38-39). But they did not yet receive the Holy Spirit, as explained in John 7:38-39.

Finally, just before returning to heaven, Jesus breathed on them and said, "Receive the Holy Spirit". It was at this time that Jesus gave them the power to forgive sins (John 10:19-22). He had made that promise to them back in Matthew 16:19 and 18:18. (Yes, the power was not given just to Peter, but to all of them.)

Even then, it was not the baptism of the Holy Spirit. In Acts 1:2-5, moments before he ascended to heaven, he told his apostles they would receive the baptism of the Holy Spirit in Jerusalem. When the wind filled the whole house where they were, they were immersed in the Holy Spirit. The word "wind" in Greek is *pneo* referring to breath. Remember back in John 10:19-22, Jesus breathed on them to give them special powers of the Holy Spirit. Now they were immersed in the breath of God, in the Holy Spirit

## UNIQUE ABILITIES

*Acts 4:5-8; Acts 5:3-9; Acts 8:13-18; Acts 16:6-7;*
*Acts 19:2-7; Ephesians 3:3-5*

There were certain unique abilities the apostles had that no one else in the church had. After all, spreading the gospel to the world began with just these twelve men.

1.    The Holy Spirit told them what to say. When they appeared before the Sanhedrin (Jewish ruling body) for preaching Jesus had come back to life and was the Son of God, Peter was filled with the Holy Spirit (Acts 5:8) and told them "You crucified Jesus" and "You killed Jesus". They got both the words and the courage to say these words from the Holy Spirit.

This fulfilled what Jesus had promised them back in Matthew 10:17-20, saying they would be taken before governors and kings and the Spirit would **tell them what to speak.**

2.    The Holy Spirit also gave them the power to **know when people were lying** (Acts 5:3) and they could even strike people dead who they believed were leading the church astray (Acts 5:5,10). They did not die in the spirit. They were not slain in the spirit. Their spirits were already dead before they came to see the apostles. At this time, they died physically.

3.    The apostles had the power to **give the Holy Spirit** separate from baptism. Remember, Acts 2:38 where Peter and the other apostles told people to repent and be baptized for the forgiveness of sins and to receive the gift of the Holy Spirit. That's what typically happens at our baptism. But early in the church, there were people who did not know the Holy Spirit existed. So the apostles had the power to give the Holy Spirit separately by laying on their hands as they did in Samaria (Acts 8:13-18) and Ephesus (Acts 19:2-7). It never happened without an apostle.

4.    The apostles were the only ones able to **pass on the power** to perform miracles and speak in languages people had not studied.

Interestingly, the Holy Spirit also told the apostles what cities to preach in, or not preach in, as evidenced in Acts 16:6-7.

These were all unique gifts of the Holy Spirit only Jesus' apostles had.

## WITNESSES

*Acts 1:21-22; Acts 2:32-33; Acts 5:29-32; Revelation 1:4-5*

Acts 1:21-23 summarizes the qualifications of an apostle. They had to have been with Jesus since the beginning of his ministry, and they had to have seen him die, and again after he came back to life. They had to be **witnesses.**

Peter and John said they were witnesses (Acts 5:29-32). The apostle John expressed it beautifully in 1:1-5: "That which was from the beginning, which we have heard, which we have seen with our eyes, which we have looked upon, and our hands have handled, concerning the Word of life ~ the life was manifested, and we have seen, and bear **witness**, and declare to you that eternal life which was with the Father and was manifested to us ~ that which we have seen and heard we declare to you, that you also may have fellowship with us; and truly our fellowship is with the Father and with his Son, Jesus Christ."

Peter passed on these words of comfort and encouragement and praise to those who lived after that time and could not have been witnesses: "The genuineness of your faith, being much more precious than gold that perishes, though it is tested by fire, may be found to praise, honor, and glory at the revelation of Jesus Christ, who having not seen you love. Though now you do not see him, yet believing, you rejoice with joy inexpressible and full of glory" (I Peter 1:7-8).

I copied Peter's last sentence on a card about twenty years ago, and it is still on my refrigerator.

## TESTIFIERS

*John 1:32-34; John 15:24-27; Hebrews 10:15-17; I John 4:13-14;
I John 5:6-10; Revelation 19:10*

What the apostles witnessed, they testified of to others to convince them to become believers also. The apostle John said, "We **testify** of what we have seen" (I John 4:13-14). They did not just testify, but they testified the truth by the power of the Holy Spirit. Jesus said in John 14:14-17 that he would send the Helper, the Spirit of Truth who would **testify** of Jesus through them. John said they testified of what they had seen (I John 4:13-14).

## SPEAKERS

*Matthew 10:1, 19-20; Acts 2:1-6, 14; Romans 9:1; Romans 15:18-19; I Corinthians 2:12-13*

The word, *laleo*, is sometimes translated preach and sometimes speak. Jesus told his apostles that they would be taken before governors and kings, but not to worry about what they would **speak**, for the Holy Spirit would tell them what to say.

On the Day of Pentecost, the twelve apostles stood up and spoke/preached. Only Peter's sermon was recorded, but all preached. "They were all filled with the Holy Spirit and began to speak with other tongues....everyone heard **them speak** in his own language" (Acts 2:4, 6).

The miracle was not in the ears of the hearers so that one person spoke and everyone heard in their own language, as some have speculated. The hearers did not have the Holy Spirit. The speakers did. Remember, there were twelve apostles the people were listening to. We have Peter's sermon recorded, but the people asked Peter and the other apostles what to do to be saved.

There were probably half a million or more people in Jerusalem on the Day of Pentecost. Though all were not there on that street that day, there was a sizeable crowd because 3000 of them were baptized for the forgiveness of their sins and to receive the gift of the Holy Spirit (Acts 2:38).

If you analyze the nations those people were from as recorded in Acts 2, you will see there were twelve languages represented. Perhaps the apostles went up onto the rooftop of the building they were meeting in, and perhaps it was on a corner so the apostles could space themselves and speak to the people of each language.

## CONFIRMERS

Mark 16:20; I Corinthians 1:6-7; Hebrews 2:3-4

After Jesus returned to heaven, the apostles preached everywhere. Jesus was still with them, working with them to **confirm** their words with signs and miracles (Mark 16:20). We do not need this confirmation anymore because the apostles' words have been recorded in a book full of built-in confirmations.

The confirmation that is the most compelling to us today is the Old Testament prophecies of world empires collapsing, often made at the height of their power. That and the Old Testament prophecies of Jesus fulfilled centuries later are what the ordinary early Christians often used to prove to unbelievers that Jesus was the long-predicted Savior, the one who was God walking among us. We can confirm the Bible in the same way today.

## SIGNS OF

*John 14:16-18; Mark 16:19-20; Acts 2:4, 16-21; Romans 15:18-19; Hebrews 2:3-4*

II Corinthians 12:12 spells out what the signs of an apostle were: "Truly the **signs** of an apostle were accomplished among you with all perseverance, in **signs** and wonders and mighty deeds" ~ miracles. Notice, these were not signs of just an ordinary Christian, but only of an apostle.

Jesus told his apostles just prior to returning to heaven that everywhere they went, their preaching would be confirmed by accompanying **signs** (Mark 16:19-20). A sign on the Day of Pentecost is when the apostles spoke in foreign languages they had not learned. Acts 2:43 and 5:12 says the apostles continued to perform miracles as they preached.

Paul and Barnabas were later apostles (Acts 14:14), and they confirmed their messages with miraculous **signs** and wonders (Acts 14:3). Paul led Gentiles to believe in Jesus through the power of their

**signs** and miracles (Romans 15:18-19).

The apostles seem to have used miraculous signs more among the Gentiles than Jews. The Jews had the Old Testament prophecies, but the pagans did not.

Once again, we do not need those signs today because of the built-in proofs in the Bible. If all the books in the Bible coincide with all the others, then the proofs in one book are proofs for the entire Bible. If those were true, the entire Bible must be true.

# 5. Relationship With New-Testament-Times Believers in General – I
## (Before New Testament Written)

## CARRIED/TAKEN

*Acts 8:26, 39-40*

True, Philip was what we today would call a deacon, and true, he could perform miracles. It was probably when the apostles laid their hands on the "deacons" that he received his power to perform miracles. (See Acts 6:5-6.)

Acts 8:26, 39-40 says that, after Philip taught and baptized the Ethiopian official somewhere between Jerusalem and Gaza, the Spirit **took** Philip to Azotus, a town about 40 miles away.

We do not know how Philip was taken, whether he walked there by compulsion of the Holy Spirit, or he suddenly was at Azotus. Either way, that's where Philip ended up because God's Spirit took him there.

## PHYSICAL

*Luke 1:35*

Mary accepted the miraculous conception of Jesus; otherwise, it would not have happened to her. Gabriel told her the Spirit would overshadow her with power (Luke 1:35).

Some of the Christians at Corinth received the gift of performing miracles from the Apostle Paul (I Corinthians 12:4). The Holy Spirit gave them the power to heal physical bodies.

As we shall see in later chapters, the Holy Spirit does both physical and spiritual things. After all, it was when the Spirit hovered over the waters covering the earth in the Beginning that the earth took form and produced all that is on earth today in preparation for God's crowning achievement, the creation of man. So, yes, the Holy Spirit can cause physical things to happen.

# GIFTS

*Acts 2:38; Acts 5:32; Acts 10:45-46; Romans 1:1, 11; I Corinthians 1:6-7; I Corinthians 12:1-9; I Corinthians 14:1; Ephesians 17-18a; Hebrews 2:3-4*

Cornelius and his household were the first Gentile Christians. The 3000 on the Day of Pentecost were the first Jewish Christians. The gift of the Holy Spirit came on Cornelius' household, and they were able to speak in other languages (Acts 10:44-45). Were they unknown languages?

When Peter reported to the leaders of the church in Jerusalem, he said the Gentiles had spoken in languages as it had happened to them at the beginning. The beginning of what? The beginning of the church. Since the apostles were understood in the languages of the people, then Cornelius and his household were understood in real languages also. God always gave the gift to encourage people to go to others who had not heard the gospel yet. More on this later.

In general, what were the special gifts of the Holy Spirit that the apostles imparted to some of the new Christians? I Corinthians 12 spells them out:

Verse 8a – Word of Wisdom. "Word" comes from the Greek *logos* meaning word or logic, that which can be known and understood. Wisdom comes from the Greek *sophia* meaning sobriety and translated elsewhere as mysterious wisdom. I Corinthians 1:18 and 30 refer to wisdom as Jesus our salvation. It applies to teaching the gospel.

Verse 8b – Word of Knowledge. In Greek, it is *logos* of *gnosis* which is that which can be understood. It is used in Colossians 1:19 as knowledge of God's will. Basically, it is how to apply God's will to our everyday life.

Verse 9a – Faith. This comes from the Greek word *pistis* meaning faithfulness. It was used by Jesus when he referred to a faith that could move mountains (Matthew 17:19-21). So, when others become discouraged, a person with this gift would be able to encourage others.

Verse 9b – Healing. This word in the Greek is *anaeros*. Besides curing diseases, the gift also refers to the maimed (people with missing arms and legs) who were made whole again instantly. The maimed are referred to in Matthew 15:30-31, and 18:8.

Verse 10a – Miracles. Miracles included raising the dead. Irenaeus, who wrote about 85 years after Revelation was written said this: So far are they from raising the dead, as the Lord raised, and as the apostles by means of prayer, for even among the brethren frequently in a case of necessity when a whole church united in much fasting and prayer, the spirit has returned to the ex-animated body, and the man was granted to the prayers of the saints....And moreover, as we said above, even the dead have been raised and continued with us many years. (See *Against Heresies* I.x.1, and *Refutation and Overthrow of False Doctrine*, Bk. 2.) If a person was given the gift of miracles by one of the apostles as a young man, he could very possibly be still doing so during the lifetime of Irenaeus.

Verse 10b – Prophecy. We have already discussed in earlier chapters that prophecy is God pouring his word into someone for them to speak. This was important before the New Testament was written.

Verse 10c-Discerning Spirits is from the Greek word *diakrisis*, referring to judging thoughts and attitudes.

Verse 10d – Different kinds of tongues. In Greek it is *diairesis*, meaning divisions of languages. (More on this later.)

Verse 10e – Interpreting tongues. This word in Greek is *diermaneuw* and does not refer to translating. It refers to explaining something thoroughly, like a commentary.

# 6. Inch-by-Inch Study of Tongues

## GLOSSA

*Mark 16:14-18; Acts 2:4; Acts 2:7-11; Acts 2:37; Acts 10:46; Romans 3:13-14; Philippians 2:11; James 1:26; James 3:5; I John 3:18*

Ten scriptures use the Greek term, *glossa* in the New Testament. Sometimes it is translated tongues and sometimes languages

In Mark 16:14-18, Jesus told his eleven remaining apostles to go into all the world to preach and baptize, and they would be helped with being able to speak in other languages and survive snake bites and poison by their enemies who follow them around.

Acts 2 refers to the tongues as being languages which everyone heard and understood. In the NIV, it identifies those who spoke in the different languages as men (see verses 7 and 15) and apostles (verses 14 and 37). If you analyze the languages represented that day, you will see there were twelve. Apparently, all the apostles spoke (there were around half a million Jews in Jerusalem that day ~ see Josephus), but only Peter's sermon was recorded.

In Acts 10:45f, the people in Cornelius' household began speaking in tongues. The word "heard" is from the Greek *akouo*, which means to harken with understanding.

In Acts 19:6, when the Ephesians spoke in tongues, the Greek word used was *laleo*, meaning to tell something or converse. One cannot have a conversation with someone they don't understand.

Romans 3:13f says some are using their tongues to practice deceit. Philippians 2:11 says every tongue will confess Jesus is Lord. James 1:26 and 3:5 say we are to bridle our tongue. I John 3:18 says we are to love in both tongue and deed.

## BABBLE AND GROANINGS

*Matthew 6:7; Acts 17:18; Romans 8:26; I Timothy 6:20;*

*II Timothy 2:16*

The word translated "vain repetitions" in Matthew 6:7 comes from the Greek word *batto-logeo*, meaning empty words. When Paul was accused in Athens of being a babbler in Acts 17:18, they used *sperma-logos*, meaning to nit pick at scraps of food with no real meat to them. Paul urged Timothy in I Timothy 6:20 and II Timothy 2:16 to avoid profane and idle babblings, using the Greek word *keno-phonia*, meaning empty sounds.

Groanings is found in Romans 8:26 regarding prayers which go so deep, they cannot be expressed. The Greek word for "groanings" is *stenagmos*, meaning to sigh. This word also appears in Acts 7:34 where Stephen said God heard the groanings of his enslaved people in Egypt.

# I CORINTHIANS

Before we take a detailed look at I Corinthians 14, let us examine why Paul wrote this letter in the first place. This congregation was full of problems. Chloe's household reported to Paul there were divisions (1:10,11). They were acting like babies (3:1) and being worldly (3:3). Some were puffed up and being bossy (4:6) and glorifying themselves (5:6). Their lives were full of malice and wickedness (5:8), they were doing things that were lawful, but not expedient (6:12), and in the middle of a crisis (7:26). They were seeking their own good instead of others' (10:24), their meetings were doing more harm than good (11:17), and some were acting like the Word of God originated with them (14:36). Paul said he had to write them to shame them (4:14, 18).

In chapter 7, verse one, Paul finally said, "Now for the matters, you wrote about" (NIV). Chapters 7:1ff are about marriage ("It is good for a man not to marry"), 8:1ff about idolatrous meals ("Now about food sacrificed to idols"), 9:1-3 about paying preachers ("….those who sit in judgment of me), 10:1ff about idolatrous meals continued, 11:1-16 about praying and prophesying to husband or wife at home.

In chapter 11:16 he says, "In the <u>following</u> directives....
your meetings...." (NIV). 11:17-34 is about keeping the Lord's
supper in the assembly, 12:1-31 is about spiritual gifts used in the
assembly, 13:1-13 is about love's superiority to tongues, 14:1-25 is
about tongues in the assembly, 14:26-40 is about orderliness in the
assembly, 15:1-58 is about resurrection of the dead being preached
in the assembly, and 16:1-4 is about collections in the assembly.

## All Mention of Tongues in
## I Corinthians 12 and 13

12:10 – Lists spiritual gifts. Among them are all kinds of
tongues. "Kinds of" comes from the Greek word *genos*, referring to
race and nationality. "Interpretation" is from the Greek word
*hermeneia*, meaning to explain, give a commentary.

12:28 – He lists people and their gifts. He begins with "First
of all" coming from the Greek *proton*, meaning in order of rank and
importance. The last gift mentioned is tongues.

12:30 – "Do all speak in tongues?" he asks. "Speak" is from
the Greek *laleo*, meaning to tell something.

13:1 – Paul brings up the tongues of angels. What are the languages
of angels? There are 15 places in the Bible where an angel spoke to
someone. Here they are, listing both the scripture where the angel
spoke to them and the scripture identifying their nationality:

Genesis 16:7-12 – Hagar – Genesis 16:3 says she was Egyptian, so
she spoke Egyptian.
Genesis 19:10-21 – Lot's Family – Genesis 11:31 says they were
Chaldean and lived in Canaan. So they spoke Aramaic or Hebrew.
Genesis 21:14-18 – Hagar – Genesis 16:3 says she was Egyptian, so
she spoke Egyptian
Genesis 22:1-2 – Abraham – Genesis 11:31 says he was Chaldean
and lived in Canaan, so he spoke Aramaic or Hebrew.
Exodus 3:1-3 – Moses – Exodus 1:15; 2:9-10 says he lived in Egypt
near Hebrews, so he spoke Egyptian and maybe Hebrew.
Judges 13:2-17 – Samson's Parents – Judges 13:1 says they were

Israelite, so they spoke Hebrew.

II Kings 1:3-4 – Elijah – I Kings 17:1 says he lived in Israel.

Daniel 8:16-25; 9:21-27 – Daniel – Daniel 1:1-4 says he was from Jerusalem and lived in Babylon, so he spoke Hebrew and Aramaic.

Luke 1:8-20 – Zechariah, John's Father – Luke 1:5 says he lived in Judea, so he spoke Hebrew and Aramaic.

Luke 1:28-38 – Mary – Luke 1:26 says she lived in Nazareth, a town of Galilee, so she spoke Aramaic.

Luke 2:8-12 – Shepherds – Luke 2:4 says they lived in Judea, so they spoke Aramaic.

Matthew 28:1-7 – Mary Magdalene & other women – Mary lived in Magdala in the province of Galilee, so she spoke Aramaic.

Acts 10:1-8 – Cornelius – Acts 10:1 says he was Italian, so he spoke Latin.

Acts 12:5-10 – Peter – John 1:44 says he was from Bethsaida, a city in the province of Galilee, so he spoke Aramaic.

Revelation 5:2, etc. – John – Matthew 4:18-21 says he lived in Galilee, so he spoke Aramaic.

What can we conclude was the tongues of angels? It was the language of whoever they spoke to.

13:8 – This says prophesy, tongues, and inspired knowledge will cease. The Greek word here is *pauomai* and is the same word used by Jesus in Luke 8:24 for the storm ceasing.

## Eusebius

Eusebius, who wrote a history of the church around 300 AD, cited Irenaeus (b.c. 120 AD) as follows: "Even down to his times, instances of divine and miraculous power were remaining in some churches....who have prophetic gifts and speak in all tongues...to expound the mysteries of God. These gifts of different kinds also continued with those that were worthy until the times mentioned" (*Eusebius' Ecclesiastical History*, Chap. VII, pg. 186-187).

Then in chapter XVI, he said a man named Montanus was "carried away in spirit and wrought up into a certain kind of frenzy and irregular ecstasy, raving and speaking and uttering strange things." After going into more detail about this, he said Montanus recruited two females to join him in his "spirit of delusion, so that they also spake like the former, in a kind of ecstatic frenzy, out of all season, and in a manner strange and novel, while the spirit of evil congratulated them." He then referred to Theodotus who fell into trances and "gave himself up to the spirit of deception....he is carried away by a vehement ecstasy....involuntary madness. They will never be able to show that any of the Old or any of the New Testament were thus violently agitated and carried away in spirit."

# I Corinthians 14

The word "tongue" is translated "languages." And remember, this is in the context of their assembly which was "doing more harm than good" (11:17).

14:1 – Paul explains that the most-desired spiritual gift should be prophecy. Remember, prophecy means pouring out God's Word, and was critically important because the New Testament was not yet written.

14:2 – Anyone speaking in a language in the assembly does not speak to men but to God because no one understands him. Indeed, if someone began speaking Persian in this Greek city, probably no one would understand them.

14:3 – Everyone who prophesies speaks to everyone.

14:4 – But anyone who speaks in a foreign language is only selfishly showing off.

14:5 – Paul wished everyone could speak in languages, but it was much more important to pour out the Word of God to people. However, if someone insisted on speaking in a language, someone had to both interpret the language and explain the meaning. NOTE: If you would like to test the authenticity of someone claiming to speak in tongues today, record them. Then play the recording to several people claiming the gift of interpretation, and see if they all agree.

14:6 – If someone speaks in a language it must include a

revelation, or divine knowledge, or prophecy.

14:7 – Even lifeless musical instruments have no meaning unless they play a tune and not the same few notes all the time.

14:8 – If a trumpet doesn't play a certain tune, no one will get ready for battle.

14:9 – So, too, if someone speaks unknown words, how will anyone know what you are trying to tell them?

14:10 – There are all kinds of languages in the world, and none of them is babbling.

14:11 – If someone in the assembly doesn't grasp the meaning of what someone is saying, he's just like a foreigner.

14:12 – Spiritual gifts must be used to instruct and improve the church.

14:13 – Therefore, if anyone speaks in a language, he should pray for the gift of explaining himself. This is the same word used in Luke 24:17 where Jesus expounded to them what was said in the prophecies about him. This word was also used in the Greek version of the Old Testament (Septuagint) in Nehemiah 8:8 where they read from the Law of Moses, making it clear and giving the meaning so the people could understand what was being read.

14:14 – If someone prays in a language, his spirit may pray, but his mind isn't influenced to apply it to his life. The word "mind" here is from the Greek word *nous*, meaning to understand. It is used in Luke 24:45 where Jesus opened their minds so they could understand the scriptures (they knew the words, but didn't know how to apply them), in Romans 1:28 regarding retaining the knowledge of God, in Romans 14:5 regarding each one being fully convinced, and Revelation 13:18 regarding having insight. The word "unfruitful" here is from the Greek *akarpos* used in the following verses: Matthew 13:22 where wealth, etc. choked out the Word of God from hearts, Ephesians 5:3-11 where immorality, greed, etc. put them in darkness, II Peter 1:5-8 where they were kept from ineffective and unproductive lives, and Jude 10-12 where heretics were referred to as clouds without rain and uprooted trees without fruit.

14:15 – In the assembly, we are to pray with both our spirit and mind and sing with our spirit and mind.

14:16 – If you are praying only with your spirit in another language, no one is going to understand you.

14:17 – If you are praying or singing in another language, no one else is encouraged.

14:18 – Paul spoke in languages more than all of them. Paul was a missionary who traveled everywhere preaching. Acts 17:6, Romans 1:8; 10:18, and Colossians 1:23, the gospel had gone to the whole world, every nation under heaven. According to secular history, Andrew went to Greece, Peter went to the Middle East and Turkey, Thaddeus went to Russia, Thomas went to India, Philip went to Turkey, Nathaniel went to Russia, Matthew went to Ethiopia and Egypt, and Simon went to Great Britain. They needed and used their gift of languages in these different nations.

14:19 – But in the church among his brethren, Paul said he'd rather speak five words everyone could understand than 10,000 words in a language.

14:20 – Now he bawls them out for acting like children.

14:21 –Here Paul quotes Isaiah 28:11-12 saying that God would speak through foreigners of strange languages.

14:22 – Therefore, languages are to be used as a sign, not among believers, but among unbelievers who wonder how they learned their language so quickly.

14:23 – If people of a congregation are speaking in different languages and an unbeliever comes to visit, he will think they are out of their mind.

14:24-25 – But, if an unbeliever comes to visit and everyone is prophesying (pouring out God's Word), he will be convinced he is a sinner and will decide God is really among them.

14:26 – If people of a congregation insist on showing off their gift of languages, prophecy, etc., there must be made a way to use these to encourage the church.

14:27 – If some insist on speaking in a foreign language, it must be one at a time, and there must be an interpreter to explain the meaning.

14:28 – If there are no interpreters, the one wanting to speak in a foreign language must remain quiet.

14:29 –Two or three prophets may speak, but the other prophets (see v. 32) must weigh carefully what has been said.

14:30 – If a revelation comes to someone who is sitting down, the speaker must stop talking and listen.

14:31 – All prophecy must be done in turns, so the congregation is instructed and encouraged.

14:32 – The prophets should monitor each other.

# 7. Relationship with New-Testament-Times Believers in General II
## (Before New Testament Written)

## Came/Fell UPON

*Acts 10:44-46; Acts 11:15-16; Acts 19:2-7*

God's Spirit **fell upon** Cornelius' household (Acts 10:44-48), and the Jews who had come with Peter were astonished. Up to then, they had thought Christianity was an offshoot of the Jewish religion; so they were amazed that God's sign of approval **fell upon** Gentiles (non-Jews) also.

In fact, when Peter reported what had happened to the leaders of the church in Jerusalem, he had to defend himself. He said in Acts 11:15 that the Holy Spirit **fell upon** them "as it had us in the beginning." The beginning of what? The Greek word he used here was *arche*. It was employed in the following four instances mentioned in the New Testament:

1.  Creation of the world: Matthew 19:4,8; 24:21; Mark 10:6; 13:19; John 1:1-2; 6:64; 8:44; Hebrews 1:10; 7:3; II Peter 3:4; I John 3:8; Revelation 1:8; 3:14; 21:6; 22:13.

2.  Beginning of Jesus' Ministry: Mark 1:1; Luke 1:2-3; John 2:11; 6:64; 8:25; 15:27; 16:4; Colossians 1:18, I John 1:1.

3.  Becoming a Christian: Acts 11:15-16; Philippians 4:15; Hebrews 3:14; I John 2:7,13, 24; 3:11; II John 5,6

4.  Beginning of the End of the World: Matthew 24:8; Mark 13:8; Revelation 1:8; 21:6; 22:13

Since Peter and the church leaders were not alive for the creation, did not have the Holy Spirit at the beginning of Jesus' ministry, and the end of the world has not begun, the only conclusion we can draw is that "on us at the beginning" was when people first became Christians at the beginning of the church in Acts 2.

Then Peter quoted Jesus as saying the apostles would be baptized with the Holy Spirit. Remember when the Day of Pentecost came, there was a rushing mighty wind that they were immersed in, and then the tongues as of fire came, then they began speaking in languages they had not studied. This had happened only to Jews.

Apparently, not only did Cornelius' family begin speaking in languages, but the wind and tongues as of fire must have also come to them. This time it happened, not to Jews, but to Gentiles (Acts 10:45). Christianity was not to be a sect of the Jews, but independent of all other religions. Peter concluded to the church leaders, "Who was I to withstand God?"

## FILLED/FULL

*Luke 1:15; Luke 1:4142; Luke 1:67; Acts 4:23-24, 31;*
*Acts 6:3, 5, 6; 8:5; Acts 7:55*

John the Baptist was **filled** with God's Spirit from the time of his birth (Luke 1:15-17). He was a miracle baby. John's mother, Elizabeth, was **filled** with the Spirit when she praised Mary and her miracle baby. John's father, Zechariah, was **filled** with the Spirit when he praised God for visiting his people and redeeming them (his prophecy about Jesus, the miracle baby).

The apostles were arrested by the Sanhedrin, then out talked their judges with the help of the Holy Spirit. As a result of hearing about this, the Christians in the congregation there in Jerusalem were **filled** with the Holy Spirit who helped them speak the Word of God with boldness (Acts 4:23-24, 31). Notice, God did not take away their enemies. Also notice that God gave them boldness, not courage. There is a difference. Courage is used when we are fearful. Boldness is used when there is no thought of danger.

The Holy Spirit **filled** Stephen so that he could be **filled** with faith (Acts 6:3-5, 8). Some people lose faith when things go wrong, but Stephen had the kind of faith that was steadfast. Surely he was a great encourager to other Christians. When he was arrested and refused to back down before the Sanhedrin, he saw their anger and that they had murder in their eyes. No one had died because of being a Christian yet; the apostles had been threatened and even imprisoned, but they had always escaped death. That was not to be for Stephen. He was about to be the first Christian to be tortured and killed for his faith. So he was **filled** with the Holy Spirit, and God gave him a glance into heaven and into the eyes of his Savior (Acts 7:55-58). With this reassurance of where he would be within the hour, he endured to the end.

God's Spirit **filled** Philip and gave him the desire to proclaim Christ (Acts 6:3-5; 8:5). He had a burden for lost souls.

So, we see here that being filled with the Holy Spirit gave miraculous physical abilities, as well as the capacity to have faith and speak to others of that faith.

## PROPHESY/SPEAK

*Luke 1:63, 67; Acts 2:16-18; Acts 19:5-6; Acts 21:8-11;*
*I Corinthians 12:3, 7, 10; Ephesians 5:18-19; Revelation 19:10*

As noted before, the Greek word for "prophecy" is *naba*, meaning to abundantly and utterly pour out. Read Jeremiah 20:9 to see how urgently the prophets poured out the words of God.

Zechariah, the father of John the Baptizer, was struck dumb for nine months. Why? He had trouble believing God was now going to answer his prayer and he would actually be having a son in his old age. But at the end of that time when God made it possible for him to talk again, all the pent-up praise he felt for God **poured out** of him as he **prophesied** about the coming Savior.

Some **prophets** from Jerusalem (where the apostles were headquartered) went to Antioch which was situated in northern Syria, near the border of today's Turkey. One of those prophets, Agabus, by the power of God's Spirit, **prophesied** and told them there was going to be a great famine throughout the world (Acts 11:27-28). With this knowledge, when Paul went on his missionary journey, he collected funds from various congregations he established to take back to the church in Jerusalem which was especially hard hit (probably also due to persecution by the Jews there ~ loss of jobs, etc.).

Twelve men in Ephesus had been baptized but did not know the Holy Spirit existed. So the apostle Paul went to them, baptized them in the name of the Lord Jesus, and gave them the Holy Spirit separate from baptism. Of course, the apostles were the only ones who could give the Holy Spirit separate from baptism as explained in Acts 2:38.

Then they were able to speak in languages they had not studied, and to **prophecy** (Acts 19:1-7). These men lived in today's Turkey, far from Jerusalem, the hub of the church at that time. Ephesus was a great seaport, and people of many languages stopped there. These twelve Gentiles were equipped to teach them the Word of God among their people.

The church at Corinth had several prophets. It was Paul who confirmed his message about Christ to them by giving them spiritual gifts, including that of **prophecy** (I Corinthians 1:1, 6-7). He gave them this gift of prophecy for the common good of their congregation (I Corinthians 13:8). All their gifts, including that of prophecy, were given by the same Spirit (I Corinthians 12:4-9).

Throughout I Corinthians 12, Paul explained that there are many gifts of the Holy Spirit, but the ones that are not showy are the most important (verses 22-24). We can't see our heart or brain, but they are necessary for life. We can see eyes and ears, arms and legs, but they are not necessary for life. Prophecy is not necessarily made before a large group. In fact, we see examples of ordinary Christians prophesying to a small group, or even just one person. Zechariah prophesied before family members and close friends (Luke 1:58-79). Elizabeth prophesied to Mary (Luke 1:40-45). Mary prophesied to Elizabeth (Luke 1:46-55). Agabus prophesied to people at the Antioch congregation (Acts 11:27-28). Philip's daughters were prophetesses (Acts 21:9), but we have no record of who they prophesied to.

Today, we have the scriptures. Peter said in II Peter 1:20 that scripture is prophecy. Once the New Testament was written, we no longer needed the gift of prophecy. It eventually faded away (I

Corinthians 13:8).

Some people claim today to have the gift of prophecy. In that case, they have knowledge of scriptures that no one else has. After the New Testament was written once for al, it would be unfair to give more scripture to one and not everyone. Paul called this having another gospel, which is no gospel at all (Galatians 1:6-9).

# 8. Inch-by-Inch Study of Acts 2 Prophecies

There is a lot of misunderstanding about that portion of Peter's sermon on the Day of Pentecost when he quoted the prophet Joel. Let us go sentence by sentence and even phrase by phrase in Acts 2:16-21 to discover what he was telling them.

Remember, everyone out in the streets near the house where the apostles were, heard the sound of the mighty rushing wind (verses 1-6a). Apparently, the apostles all rushed out of the house to praise God, either onto the street or onto the rooftop, for the crowd heard them and were amazed because everyone heard the apostles in their native language (verses 6b-12).

When you look at the parts of the world that were represented in the crowd and analyze their languages, you will find twelve languages ~ one for each apostle. Apparently, some in the crowd were trying to listen to all the apostles, not just the one who spoke their language; and the other languages sounded like gibberish to them. Rather than listen to the apostle who spoke their language and find out what they were trying to tell them, the scoffers just accused them of being drunk (verse 13).

Apparently, all of the apostles gave a sermon, but only Peter's was recorded. Remember, they ended up baptizing 3,000, so must have had an audience of tens of thousands at least. Peter told them they were not drunk, but what they had seen and heard was a fulfillment of the prophecy of Joel centuries earlier. That prophecy is found in Joel 2:28-3:2. Let us examine it from Peter's quote:

> *And it shall come to pass in the last days, says God,*
> *That I will pour out of My Spirit on all flesh.*
> Verses 16-17a

When were or are the last days? Hebrews 1:11-2 that "in these last days" God spoke to us through his Son, Jesus. I Peter 1:19-20 says the precious blood of Christ was poured out for mankind "in these last times." So, we must conclude that the last days began with the life and death of Jesus Christ.

*Your sons and your daughters shall prophesy.*
Verse 17b

What descendant (son) of Aaron "prophesied" about Jesus? Luke 1:5, 67 says it was Zechariah at the time of John's (the Baptist's) birth.

What other son of the Israelites "prophesied" about Jesus? Luke 2:25-35 says it was Simeon who met baby Jesus in the temple.

What descendant (daughter) of Aaron "prophesied" about Jesus? Luke 1:5, 4-45 says it was Elizabeth.

What other daughter of the Israelites "prophesied" about Jesus? Luke 2:36-38 says it was Anna who met baby Jesus in the temple.

What sons of the Israelites "prophesied" about Jesus? Acts 2:1-4 says it was the apostles of Jesus.

*Your young men shall see visions.*
*Your old men shall dream dreams.*
Verse 17c

What young man dreamed a "dream"? Matthew 1:20-23 says it was Joseph. (Note: Despite tradition from who-knows-where, Joseph was still alive during Jesus' ministry. John 6:42 mentions Joseph in the present tense. Apparently, he died a year or two before Jesus did.)

What old men dreamed the same "dream"? Matthew 2:1,12 says the Magi, the wise men, did.

What old man saw a "vision"? Luke 1:11f says Zechariah did.

*And on my menservants and on my maidservants*
*I will pour out my Spirit in those days;*
*And they shall prophesy.*
Verse 18

This is pretty much explained above.

*I will show wonders in heaven above.*
Verse 19a

What wonder occurred "above" when Jesus was born? Luke 2:8-15 says angels appeared from heaven to the shepherds.

What other wonder occurred "above" when Jesus was born? Matthew 2:1-2, 9-10 says the wise men saw the star over Bethlehem.

What wonder occurred "above" when Jesus was baptized? Matthew 3:16-17 says the heavens were opened and the Spirit of God descended like a dove and alighted on Jesus, and God spoke.

What wonder occurred "above" when Jesus was praying on the mountain? Matthew 17:1-5 says Elijah and Moses appeared to Jesus, then a cloud from heaven engulfed them all.

What wonder occurred "above" when Jesus was preaching in the temple? John 12:28f says God's thunderous voice declared his glory.

What wonder occurred "above" during Jesus' last few moments with his apostles? Acts 1:9 says he ascended to heaven.

What wonder occurred "above" on the Day of Pentecost? Acts 2:2 says a great sound came down from heaven like a rushing, mighty wind.

*And signs in the earth beneath:*
Verse 19b

What signs "on earth" were the shepherds given? Luke 2:12 says the Savior of the world would be wrapped in swaddling bands and lying in an animal's feed trough.

What sign "on earth" did Jesus say the wicked would see? Matthew 12:39-40 says Jesus would only be buried three days.

What sign "on earth" occurred after Jesus' death? John 20:18-28 says Jesus came out of his grave and walked the earth again.

Who performed many miraculous signs "on earth" and why? John 20:30f says Jesus did so people would believe he was the Son of God.

With what did God give accreditation to Jesus among the people "on earth"? Acts 2:22 says Jesus' apostles performed miracles, wonders, and signs.

> *Blood and fire and vapor of smoke.*
> Verse 19c

Vapor is also translated breath or wind. In the Old Testament, smoke represented the presence of God on Mount Sinai (Exodus 19:9), and Solomon's temple (II Chronicles 7:1-3).

What blood were Joel and Peter referring to? Acts 2:23 says it was the "blood" of Jesus who was crucified.

What fire were Joel and Peter referring to? Acts 2:3 says it was divided tongues like "fire" that descended on each apostle on the Day of Pentecost.

What vapor of smoke were Joel Peter referring to? Acts 2:2 says it was the rushing, mighty wind that descended on the house where the apostles were on the Day of Pentecost. The word "wind" in the Greek is *pneo*. *Pneuma* is translated spirit. Vapor is also translated breath or wind in the Bible.

> *The sun shall be turned into darkness.*
> Verse 20a

On what occasion just recently had the sun turned dark? Luke 23:44 says it was while Jesus was on the cross.

> *And the moon into blood.*
> Verse 20b

Whose blood had been spilled recently while it was dark and the moon could be seen? Luke 23:44 says it was Jesus' blood.

> *Before the coming of the great and awesome day of the Lord.*
> *And it shall come to pass*
> *That whoever calls on the name of the Lord*

*Shall be saved.*
Verse 10c & 21

Could all the animal sacrifices made in the Old Testament era save anyone? Hebrews 10:11 says no.

Who had to take on flesh to be sacrificed so we could be saved by calling on his name? Hebrews 10:10 says Jesus.

When did this turn of events occur? Acts 2:1, 38 says Peter and the other apostles told them they could have their sins washed away and receive the Holy Spirit at baptism.

# 9. Attributes of the Holy Spirit – I

Of course, some of the attributes of God the Spirit overlap with God the Father and God the Son. The differences are discussed in later chapters.

## IS CREATIVITY

*Genesis 1:1-2; Job 26:13; Psalm 51:10-12; Psalm 104:30*

The first view we have of God's Holy Spirit is in the very first verse of the very first chapter of the Bible. It describes the Spirit as hovering over the waters of the newly created dark earth, The Hebrew word for "hover" is *rachaph,* meaning to shake or tremble. It is beautifully used in Deuteronomy 32:11 where an eagle flutters her wings over her nest to protect it.

And so, once the Spirit began hovering over the earth, things started to happen. It began to take form and light came into being, and magnificent things began to appear on and above it. The mind of the Father conceived them, the Son of the Father spoke them, and the Spirit of the Father brought them into existence.

The Spirit not only was in on creating the earth, but he renews it every spring according to Psalm 104:30. Whenever we plant something, we are workers together with God's Spirit. Whenever we take something created by the Spirit and make something out of it, we are workers together with God's Spirit.

Did you ever think about the fact that God made the earth, but he left it unfinished? He left gold and silver and rubies in the earth. He left houses and dams and cities unbuilt. He left the waters unfished, and mountains unclimbed and ground untilled. He even left music unsung, poetry unwritten, and dramas unplayed. He left it all here to challenge us and turn us into dreamers and thinkers and experimenters. He left it all here so we could share in the joy of creating. Ecclesiastes flourishes with such fulfillment, and urges, "Whatever your hand finds to do, do it with your mind (Ecclesiastes 9:10).

# IS POWER
## "Willpower"

*Isaiah 11:1-2; Isaiah 63:11-14; Zechariah 4:6-10; Ephesians 6:11-12*

When the Israelites left their captivity in Babylon and returned to Jerusalem to rebuild the temple (even before rebuilding the city), they ran into obstacle after obstacle. In addition to challenges of clearing away debris and moving huge blocks of stone to put them back in place, pagan political leaders who had established themselves in the absence of the Jews interfered any way they could.

God told Zerubbabel, "Not by might nor by **power**, but by my Spirit' says the Lord of hosts....Then you will know that the Lord of hosts has sent me to you....For who has despised the day of small things?" (Zechariah 4:6-10).

Today, God's Spirit gives us the power to take on projects that seem impossible: Convert Muslims to Christ, reverse the amoral trend in America, convert stubborn relatives, change governments where Christianity is illegal. Ephesians 6:11-17 tells us what to use in these battles of will: Truth, righteousness, the gospel of peace, the helmet of salvation and the sword of the Spirit which is the Word of God.

Whenever we try, whenever we do battle in our own weak way, that is the Holy Spirit in us. How do we know? Because the Bible says so. It's not a feeling; it is knowing.

When we struggle with personal weaknesses as Paul explained in Romans 7, and our flesh is warring with our mind, God's Spirit helps us. The conclusion to the struggle Paul spoke of is in Romans 8:1: "There is no condemnation to those who walk in the Spirit." Therefore, whenever we overcome a bad habit or attitude, that is the Holy Spirit's power in us. The Spirit gives us the power to be like Jesus. So whenever we do become more like Jesus, that is the Holy Spirit in us.

# IS LIFE

*Job 27:3; 33:4; Ecclesiastes 12:7; Ezekiel 37:11-14; Luke 2:25-27; Luke 9:54-56; John 6:58, 63; John 7:38-39; Acts 2:32-33; Acts 11:9,12; Acts 16:6-10; Romans 6:4-6; 8:3-4; Romans 8:5-13; II Corinthians 3:3, 6; II Corinthians 5:4-5, 10; Galatians 5:16, 24-25; Galatians 6:7-8; Philippians 1:19-23; Hebrews 9:14; I Peter 2:5; I Peter 3:18; I John 3:24; Revelation 5:6; Revelation 22:17*

## Given As Promised

Job explained in 27:3 and 33:4 that the Spirit of God made him, and the breath of God gives him **life.** Ecclesiastes 12:7 is often quoted: "Then the dust return to the earth as it was, and the spirit will return to God who gave it."

Acts 2 quotes the prophet Joel 2:28-32 and concludes that whoever calls on the name of the Lord will be saved. Saved from what? Eternal death. Saved for what? Eternal **life.** Joel said God would pour out his Spirit on all nations; not everyone in them, but everyone in the nations who accept him.

How do we accept him? Acts 2:38 says we are to repent and be baptized for the forgiveness of our sins, and we will receive the gift of the Holy Spirit. What is the gift? Life and all the other attributes of God's Spirit. Romans 6:3-4 explains it further: When we are baptized, we are born again unto a new **life.**

## In Our Daily Life

"Clearly you are an epistle of Christ, ministered by us, written not with ink, but by the Spirit of the living God, not on tablets of stone but on tablets of flesh, that is, of the heart....not of the letter but of the Spirit; for the letter kills, but the Spirit gives **life**" (II Corinthians 3:3, 6). Edgar A. Guest wrote the now-famous poem for the *Detroit Free Press* entitled, "I'd Rather See a Sermon than hear one any day."

Jesus said in John 7:38-39 that **living** water came out of him, and would also flow out of our hearts, explaining further that he was referring to the Spirit who would be given to all believers. How is it possible for waters of life to flow from us? By imitating Jesus. Jesus never waited for a committee or a synagogue to officially endorse something. He just went out and did things. He went out to "seek and save the lost" (Luke 19:10) and to help the suffering with his miracles. It was not something added to his daily life; it was who he was.

Paul explained in Romans 8:5-13 that we must live by the Spirit, for to be spiritually minded is **life** and peace. The same Spirit that raised Jesus from the dead gives **life** to our mortal bodies.

I Peter 3:5 explains that we are made up of **living** stones, a spiritual house, and holy priests offering up spiritual sacrifices. Romans 12:1 further illustrates that we are to offer our bodies as **living** sacrifices. Whenever we do good works, that is the Holy Spirit in us. How do we know? Because the Bible says so.

### In Eternity

Jesus explained in John 6:58, 63 that, if we eat the bread of life, we will **live** forever, for "It is the Spirit who gives **life**…The words I speak to you are spirit, and they are life."

When we die, death is swallowed up by **life.** God has given us his Spirit as a guarantee this will happen (II Corinthians 5:4-10) In Revelation 22:17 we are reassured, for the Spirit and bride invite Jesus to return for us. Where is the Spirit? On earth with the bride. Who is the bride? The church.

## IS HEART

*Genesis 6:3-6; Ezekiel 11:19-20; Ezekiel 36:26-27; Romans 5:5; Romans 15:30; II Corinthians 1:21-22; II Corinthians 3:3; II Corinthians 13:14; Galatians 4:6; Galatians 5:22-24; Philippians 2:1-2; Colossians 1:8; II Timothy 1:7*

When someone has heart, that someone reacts to things and creates self-motivation to say and do things. During the disastrous days before the flood, God said, "My Spirit shall not strive with man forever....the thoughts of his heart were only evil continually....and he [God] was grieved in his **heart**" (Genesis 6:3-6).

Ezekiel 36:26-27 says God was going to put a new **heart** in people along with his Spirit to cause people to keep his commandments. Yes, heart isn't just an emotion; it is more of a reaction that creates motivation. When we have a new heart by the Spirit, it is God's Spirit that is now living in our heart. If we react to things the way God does, his heart is in us.

Galatians explains that, because we are sons of God, he has sent forth his Spirit into our **hearts** so that we can call God our Father. If we respect our father, how do we treat him? If we love our father, how do we treat him? II Corinthians 1:21-22 reassures us that God has given us his Spirit in our hearts as a guarantee of our salvation. How do we know? Jesus promised in John 14:17 that he was going to send us the Spirit of Truth. And what is the Spirit of Truth? John 17:17 says God's Word is Truth. So, if God's Word is in our heart, we know that God's Spirit is there.

# IS MIND

*I Chronicles 28:11-12; Isaiah 40:13-14; Ezekiel 11:5; John 14:17, 26; 17:17; Romans 8:5-6, 27; I Corinthians 2:14-15; I Corinthians 12:7-8*

The Holy Spirit thinks. Some religions claim a god who does not think; their god is just existence, the essence of the universe. Brahman. Nirvana. Our God has a mind and uses it to communicate with us.

I Chronicles 28:11-12 refers to the plans for the temple which David had "by the Spirit." Jesus explained in John 14:16, 26; and 17:17 that he would send the Spirit of Truth who will teach them all things, and bring to their remembrance everything Jesus had taught them.

Paul explains in Romans 8:5-6 that, if we live according to the Spirit, we have the **mind** of the Spirit. In 8:27 he says that God's Mind communicates with our mind through the Spirit, but only if we are living in the will of God.

# IS WISDOM

*Genesis 41:38-39; Deuteronomy 34:9; Job 32:7-8; Proverbs 1:20, 23; Isaiah 11:1-2; Acts 6:3-6, 10; I Corinthians 2:4-5, 13; I Corinthians 12:8; Ephesians 1:17-18; Colossians 1:9; Colossians 3:16*

The connection of God to wisdom is often made by people referring to Proverbs 1. In verses 10 and 23, he says, "**Wisdom** calls aloud outside; she raises her voice in the open squares....Surely I will pour out my spirit on you; I will make my words known to you."

"There is a spirit in man, and the breath of the Almighty gives him understanding" (Job 32:7-8). Joshua was given the Spirit of **wisdom** (Deuteronomy 34:9). When the church was young and needing direction in feeding widows, they sought out from among their congregation seven men "full of the Holy Spirit and **wisdom**."

Paul said he did not preach with human wisdom, but what the Holy Spirit taught (I Corinthians 2:4-5, 13). Colossians refers to knowledge of God's will in all **wisdom** and spiritual understanding (3:16), and the Word of Christ dwelling in us with wisdom (3:16).

# IS THOUGHT

*Genesis 6:3-6; Proverbs 1:20-23; Mark 2:8; I Corinthians 2:9-10; I Corinthians 2:13; Hebrews 4:12-13*

Thoughts are unsaid words and un-acted-upon deeds. Proverbs 1:23 refers to God pouring out his Spirit on us with **plans** to make his words known.

I Corinthians 2:9-10 announces that God has **prepared** amazing things for those who love him. "God has revealed them to us through his Spirit. For the Spirit **searches** all things, yes, the deep things of God."

Hebrews 4:12-13 says the Word of God (remember, John 14:17 refers to the Spirit of Truth) is like a sword **discerning the thoughts** and intents of man's heart.

# 10. Attributes of the Holy Spirit – II

## PUTTING IT ALL TOGETHER

God's Holy Spirit exists in the physical realm. He is creativity. Every time we create something for godly purposes that is God's Spirit in us. He is power. Every time there was a miracle performed in the Bible or every time someone was compelled by God to be in another location, that was God's Spirit in them. Today in our daily life, every time we make a decision to do godly works, that is Gods Spirit in us.

God's Holy Spirit exists in the spiritual realm. God's Spirit provides a link between earth and heaven through his promises of heaven. In baptism, we are given the Holy Spirit (Acts 2:38) and the promise that, if we are raised out of the grave-like waters of baptism (Romans 6:3-4), we will be raised after our physical death and be taken up to heaven. Therefore, the Spirit is life. Why? Because the Spirit is also love.

God's Holy Spirit exists in the mental realm. He is the mind of Christ (I Corinthians 2:14-15). He is wisdom. He is the motivator. He is all godly thought.

We have seen how God's Spirit went from physical to spiritual to mental. Now we shall see how he returns to the physical ~ full circle.

What is in the Mind of God's Spirit? What are the Spirit's thoughts? They are truth, which becomes Word, which becomes the Spirit's message to us ~ the Bible (back to the physical).

Why? Because there is a great struggle between good and evil, and we are in the middle of it. Remember, Ephesians 6:12 says, "We do not wrestle against flesh and blood, but against powers, against the rulers of the darkness of this age, against spiritual hosts of wickedness in the heavenly places."

Now, look at this diagram of the circle of the Holy Spirit, reading it clockwise.

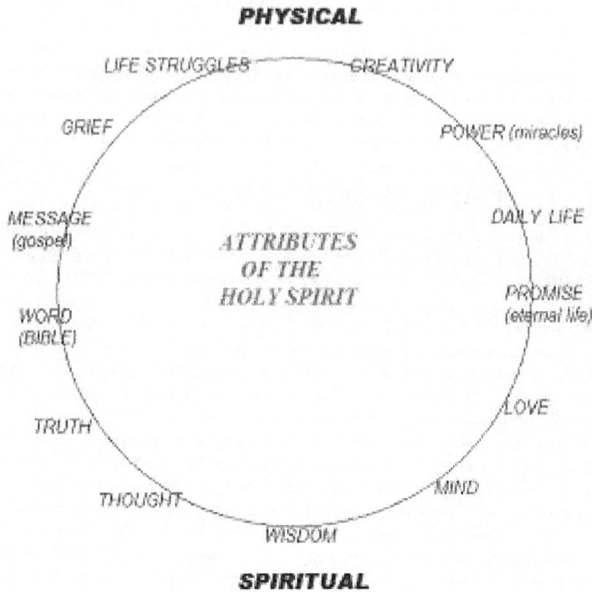

**PHYSICAL**

LIFE STRUGGLES — CREATIVITY

GRIEF                    POWER (miracles)

MESSAGE              DAILY LIFE
(gospel)

*ATTRIBUTES
OF THE
HOLY SPIRIT*                PROMISE
WORD                    (eternal life)
(BIBLE)

                                LOVE

TRUTH

THOUGHT                    MIND

WISDOM

**SPIRITUAL**

# TRUTH

*John 3:5; John 4:23-24; John 13:21; John 14:17; 17:1; John 15:26;
Romans 9:1; Galatians 5:5-10; Ephesians 1:13-14;
II Thessalonians 2:8-10, 13; I Timothy 4:1-3; Hebrews 10:26-29; I John
4:6; I John 5:6*

Jesus was born into our world to bear witness to the truth (John 18:36-38). Truth is the gospel of our salvation (Ephesians 1:13-14). Salvation from what? Hell. Salvation to what? Heaven. Heaven is whose home? God's? God is what? Sinless. Was Jesus? Yes. Jesus was our example, our witness in the flesh of what truth is.

What is sin? Sin is anything that hurts our souls. Who determines what sin is? God who is sinless. Why? He created us and wants us to live with him.

Remember in the Garden of Eden when God said the moment

56

they sinned, they would die? Death means separation. Physical death means separation from the earth. Spiritual death means separation from God. Jesus came to live that sinless life that is impossible for us to live so he could be a witness to the truth of salvation.

# WORD

*II Samuel 23:1-2; Isaiah 40:7-8; Isaiah 59:21; Micah 2:7; Zechariah 4:6; Zechariah 7:12; Matthew 8:16; John 3:34-35; John 6:63; John 14:17; 17:17; Acts 4:31; Acts 10:44-47; Acts 13:49-52; Romans 8:26; I Corinthians 2:4, 13; Ephesians 1:13; Ephesians 1:13; Ephesians 6:17; I Thessalonians 1:5-6; Hebrews 4:12-13; Hebrews 6:4-6*

Decades ago, it was common to hear someone say the Spirit is the Word of God. It is not heard so much anymore. But let us investigate it.

Jesus said in John 14:16 and 17a, "I will pray the Father and he will give you another Helper, that he may abide with you forever ~ the Spirit of Truth." Then in John 17:17 he explains, "Sanctify them by your truth. Your word is truth." So there we have it. God's Spirit is manifested to us in God's Word, the Bible.

For Muslims, if the *Qur'an* is desecrated by touching it without washing hands, letting it sit on the ground or other blasphemous things, it is the same thing as blaspheming Allah, because the *Qur'an* is the incarnation of Allah.

In Christianity, Jesus was the incarnation of God. Jesus was the Word (John 1:1,2,14). The Bible is the incarnation of Jesus, the Word of God. Jesus was God the Word we could see. The Holy Spirit is God the Word we can read.

# MESSAGE/SPEECH

*Numbers 11:16-17; Ezekiel 2:2-3; Ezekiel 3:24-27; Matthew 10:1, 18-20; Matthew 12:30-32; Matthew 22:43-44; John 3:34;*

*Acts 1:16; Acts 2:1-4, 6-7, 14; Acts 23:1, 9; Romans 9:1; Romans 15:18-29; I Corinthians 2:4, 12-13;*
*I Corinthians 12:3, 8, 10; Ephesians 5:18-19; I Peter 1:10-12; Revelation 2:7, 11, 17*

Jesus said in Matthew 12:30-32 that the one sin that is unforgivable is blaspheming the Holy Spirit. When we blaspheme something, we disrespect it because we do not believe it. If we blaspheme the Holy Spirit, we blaspheme the Word of God because we do not believe it. As long as we disbelieve the Word of God, we cannot be forgiven. It is impossible.

There are forty scriptures about the Spirit's creativity, influence on our physical life, and power of miracles. There are thirty-six scriptures covering the Spirit's emotions of love, heart, belief, and struggle. That is a total of seventy-six scriptures covering the physical and emotional attributes of the Holy Spirit.

There are seventy-one scriptures covering the Spirit's truth, Word, and message. There are twenty-eight scriptures covering the Spirit's mind, wisdom, and thoughts. That is a total of ninety-nine scriptures covering the Word attributes of the Holy Spirit.

# GRIEF/ANGER

*Genesis 6:3, 5-7; Judges 14:19; I Samuel 11:1, 6, 11; Isaiah 63:1, 10; Ezekiel 3:14-15; Micah 2:6-8; Zechariah 12:10; John 11:32-33; Acts 5:1-5; Ephesians 4:30-31; I Thessalonians 5:19-20; Hebrews 10:25-29*

What is God's Spirit grieved at? Sin. Why? Because sin separates us from God. Remember in Genesis 6:3 and 6, God said, "My Spirit shall not strive with man forever....The Lord was sorry he had made man on the earth, and he was **grieved** in his heart."

Isaiah explained God's reactions to the Israelites who had "rebelled and **grieved** his Holy Spirit" (63:1,10). Paul urges us to not "**grieve** the Holy Spirit of God" when we express bitterness, wrath, anger, clamor, evil speaking, and malice (Ephesians 4:30-31).

That means every time we grow bitter because other people in the congregation do not accept our suggestions, every time we complain about it, and every time our heart turns to malice for them, we are grieving God's Spirit.

He does not want his children to fight among themselves. There is evil out there we must be fighting. If we are busy fighting evil, we will not have time to fight among ourselves.

## STRUGGLE/WARNING

*Acts 16:6-10; Acts 20:17, 28; Acts 20:22-23; Romans 8:26;*
*I Corinthians 2:4, 13; Ephesians 1:13; Ephesians 6:17;*
*I Thessalonians 1:5; Hebrews 4:12-13; Hebrews 6:4-6;*
*Hebrews 9:1, 8-10*

We are in a daily struggle. It's not just with other people or with our own bad habits. It is really a struggle against "principalities, against powers, against the rulers of the darkness of this age, against spiritual hosts of wickedness in the heavenly places" (Ephesians 6:12).

How do we know how to struggle? We use the sword of the Spirit, the Word of God (Ephesians 6:17), the precious, valiant, stronger-than-we-are Word of God.

So, every time we give in to self-pity or self-arrogance, every time we give in and fight or argue with someone who wants to fight or argue with us, Satan wins, and God loses. But, every time we rise above them and think and act on "whatever things are noble, whatever things are just, whatever things are pure, whatever things are lovely, whatever things are of good report" (Philippians 4:8), Satan loses, and God wins.

Whose side are you on?

# 11. Relationship With Believers After the New Testament Was Written-I

We are particularly interested in this topic because this is how God's Holy Spirit affects those of us born after the New Testament was written. Remember, all the miracles were performed to confirm the words orally spoken were really from God (John 20:30-31, and elsewhere). I Corinthians 13:8 explains, "Love never fails. But whether there are prophecies, they will fail; whether there are tongues, they will cease; whether there is [miraculous] knowledge, it will vanish away."

So, what's left for us in our present age? Plenty. That's why this subject will take two chapters.

## SIN

We need our sins washed away. If we think we're "not so bad," think again. There are thirteen lists of sins scattered throughout the New Testament: Romans 1:29-31; I Corinthians 6:9-10; Galatians 5:19-21; Ephesians 4:31, 5:4f; Philippians 2:3,14; Colossians 3:8-9; I Timothy 1:9-10, 5:13, 6:3-5; II Timothy 3:2-8; Titus 3:3, 9-11; James 3:1-16, 4:1-3, 5:3-6; I Peter 2:1, 4:3; II Peter 2:14-19; Jude 7, 8, 16; Revelation 21:8.

We may not murder and steal, but we do sin. Sins listed in the Bible include things like envy, greed, gossip, boastfulness, slander, bitterness, foolish talk, coarse joking, selfishness, conceit, complaining, arguing, lying, pride, deceit, lust, faultfinding, flattery, lying, and even being a coward. That's just some of them. Been doing any of them lately? We all have. We do them nearly every day.

And if that doesn't catch us all on a daily basis, this will: Sins of omission, sins of not doing good works we should be doing. Matthew 3:10 5:42, 6:1, and 25:41-45 talk about this. So do Romans 12:11-21; Ephesians 5:17-18; I Timothy 5:8; Hebrews 10:25-29, 13:2, 3, 16; and James 1:22-26 2:14-19.

We may think to ourselves, "Well, I'm generally a good person, so God will overlook this one little quirk of mine." Or, the catch-all, "If God loves me like he claims, he will surely not let me go to hell."

But heaven is God's home, not our home. Just as we have a door on our home, he has a door on his. Just as we are not required to let just anyone into our home who wants in, God is not obliged to let just anyone into his home who wants in. Just as we consider criminals people who try to break into our home their own way, God considers criminals people who try to break into his home their own way.

What God says, he means. When Abraham told a half-lie about Sarah being his sister (she was his half-sister and also his wife), Pharaoh put her in his harem, and God sent a plague on Pharaoh's house (Genesis 12:10-20). Sodom and other nearby cities were destroyed because of private acts between consenting adults ~ homosexuality (Genesis 19:5). When Abraham didn't learn his lesson and lied about his wife again, King Abimelech took her into his harem, and God told him in a dream, "You are a dead man!" (Genesis 20:2-3).

When High Priest Aaron's sons used fire from the wrong source to burn incense, the fire leaped out and burned them (Leviticus 10:1-2). When Korah led 250 men to oppose Moses, Korah was swallowed up in an earthquake (Numbers 16:1-3, 26, 32). When Moses and Aaron struck a rock to get water out of it instead of just speaking to it, God told them they would never enter the Promised Land (Deuteronomy 34:4; Numbers 20:24,28; 28:8,11-12).

Even though only men from the tribe of Levi were allowed to offer sacrifices, King Saul from the tribe of Benjamin got impatient and offered a sacrifice himself, resulting in the kingdom being taken from him (Numbers 18:1-3; I Samuel 9:1-2). Even though the Levites were to carry the Ark of the Covenant on poles, they put it on a cart for oxen to carry, resulting in people trying to steady the ark being killed (Exodus 37:3-5; Numbers 4:15; II Samuel 6:3, 6-7).

In the New Testament, Ananias and Sapphire told a lie about their contribution to the church, and they died for it (Acts 5:1-11).

61

Though the congregation in Ephesus was full of good works and proper doctrine, they weren't doing it out of love, so Jesus was about to remove their light from heaven (Revelation 2:1-5). The congregation in Pergamum had developed a system of clergy and laity, and Jesus was about to remove their light from heaven (Revelation 2:12-16). Though the congregation at Thyatira was full of good works, some were committing sexual immorality, so Jesus was about to remove their light from heaven (Revelation 2:18-29). Though the congregation in Sardis was known as a lively church, they weren't doing good works, and Jesus was about to take their light from heaven. Even the congregation at Laodicea was threatened because it was "neither hot nor cold."

So, even "little sins" we do as individuals affect others and can lead to destruction; and going with a congregation in the wrong direction can do so also.

# WASH

*Isaiah 4:2, 4; I Corinthians 6:9-11; Titus 3:3-7*

Isaiah, in 4:2-4, refers to the Branch of the Lord and says the Lord **washes** away our filth by the Spirit of judgment and burning. Burning is used elsewhere in reference to refining by burning away the excess until only that which is valuable is left.

After listing several sins which will keep us out of the kingdom of God, Paul says, "Such were some of you. But you were **washed,** but you were sanctified, but you were justified in the name of the Lord Jesus and by the Spirit of our God" (I Corinthians 6:9-11).

Once again, Paul makes a list of sins, including malice, envy and even hating each other, but then says our Savior came to us and saved us "through the **washing** of regeneration and renewing of the Holy Spirit," having been justified by God's grace (Titus 3:3-7).

Recalling his own conversion, the apostle Paul said, that he was told, "Arise and be baptized and **wash** away your sins, calling on the name of the Lord" (Acts 22:16).

What does it mean to be justified? It means to be exonerated and found not guilty.

# WATER

*Genesis 1:1-2; Isaiah 44:2-3; Matthew 3:11-12; Matthew 3:16; John 1:32-34; John 3:5-6; John 7:37-39; Acts 10:47-48; I John 5:6; Revelation 22:17*

In the Beginning, God's Spirit hovered over the earth. It is interesting that the Spirit was hovering over the **waters.** "Hovering" is from the Hebrew word *achaph*. This word is used in Deuteronomy 32:11 about a symbolic eagle protecting her nest. The earth was born out of water. It is used again in Jeremiah 23:9 where the prophet was excited over the prospect of the Messiah, the Savior of the world, being born some day.

Water seems to always be used in connection with new birth. And, so, when God's Spirit hovered over the waters of the dark earth, he was getting ready for the earth to be born out of the waters.

Water has always been a symbol of a **watery** womb and life. "I formed you from the [watery] womb....I will pour **water** on him who is thirsty, floods on the dry ground; I will pour my Spirit on your descendants" (Isaiah 44:2-3).

John the Baptist baptized people with **water** because of their repentance (Matthew 3:11) Jesus' own baptism brought even more meaning to the act. After he was baptized in **water**, the Holy Spirit descended on him (Matthew 3:16).

Finally, Jesus ties it all together in John 3:5-6: "Unless one is born of **water** AND the Spirit, he cannot enter the kingdom of God. That which is born of the flesh is flesh, and that which is born of the Spirit is spirit." Peter explained it in Acts 2:38, "Repent and be baptized [in water] for the forgiveness of your sins, and you will receive the gift of the Holy Spirit."

# SANCTIFY/SAVE/JUSTIFY

*Luke 9:54-56; Romans 15:16; I Corinthians 6:9-11;*
*II Thessalonians 2:13; Titus 3:5-6; Hebrews 10:29;*
*I Peter 1:2, 10-12*

## Saved From What?

Our view of salvation has become one-sided. We talk about being saved so we can go to heaven. But saved from what? People are saved from losing their jobs, losing their homes, losing their health. People are saved from drowning in swimming pools, from dying with antibiotics, from maiming crashes with seat belts. Being saved refers to what we are being saved from.

Christian salvation refers to being saved from hell. Just what is hell? It is the absence of heaven.

Heaven has no pain (Revelation 21:4), so hell is full of agony (Luke 16:24) and gnashing of teeth (Matthew 25:30).

Heaven has no crying (Revelation 21:4), so hell is where there will be weeping: (Luke 13:28).

Heaven has water (Revelation 22:1-2), so hell has no water (Luke 16:24).

Heaven has food (Revelation 7:16), so hell does not.

Heaven has light (Revelation 21:23), so hell is complete darkness (Matthew 25:30).

Heaven is full of activity (Revelation 7:9-10), so in hell, people are bound hand and foot and can do nothing (Matthew 22:13).

Heaven is where God remembers our sins no more (Hebrews 10:17), so hell is where Satan accuses us forever (Revelation 12:10).

The wages of sin is death (Romans 6:23). That's what we earn every day of our life because we sin every day of our life. What is death? Separation. What is the death of our souls? Separation from God and his home.

## What Then?

Paul explains in I Corinthians 6:9-11, "....But you were washed, but you were sanctified, but you were justified in the name of the Lord Jesus and by the Spirit of our God."

The word "justified" in Greek is *dikaioh*, meaning to pronounce innocent, to acquit. Amazing! We are found in God's court not guilty!

God does not want anyone to be lost but wants everyone to come to repentance (II Peter 3:9). What if our friends don't think they're guilty of anything? Or their few little sins surely wouldn't keep them out of heaven, thus decided to break in a back way into heaven instead of through the door?

## BIRTH/NEW LIFE

*John 3:5-8; Galatians 4:29*

Jesus clearly explained in John 3:5-8 the necessity of a rebirth. "Most assuredly, I say to you, unless one is **born** of water and the Spirit, he cannot enter the kingdom of God. That which is **born** of the flesh is flesh, and that which is **born** of Spirit is spirit. Do not marvel that I said to you, 'You must be **born** again.' The wind blows where it wishes, and you hear the sound of it, but cannot tell where it comes from and where it goes. So is everyone who is **born** of the Spirit."

Paul explains in Galatians 4:4-7 that "God has sent forth the Spirit of His Son into your hearts, crying out, "Abba! Father!" Later, he compares us with Ishmael who was born according to the flesh, and with Isaac who was born [miraculously] according to the Spirit.

How do we obtain the new birth? Romans 6:3-4 explains it clearly: "Or do you not know that as many of us as were baptized into Christ Jesus were baptized into his death? Therefore, we were buried with him through baptism into death, that just as Christ was raised from the dead by the glory of the Father, even so, we also should walk in **newness of life**."

## Lifted/Caught/Carried/Brought UP

*Romans 14:17-18; II Corinthians 6:1, 6; Ephesians 2:12-13, 18;*

*Ephesians 6:18; Colossians 1:2, 8;*
*Hebrews 6:4-6; Jude 1:1, 20*

You will recall in lesson two that Ezekiel was **lifted** up and saw visions, and Elijah *went* **up** to heaven. In lesson three, the apostle Paul was **caught** up to the third heaven, and the apostle John was **carried** up to the New Jerusalem.

Now it is our turn! Before we are saved, we are wandering aliens with no spiritual home or kingdom to live in. But Ephesians 2:12, 13, 18 shows us, "But now in Christ Jesus, you who once were far off have been **brought** near....for through him we both have access by one Spirit to the Father."

Can you imagine not being near God? Can you imagine being without God? How frightening! How empty!

## POUR

*Proverbs 1:20-23; Isaiah 32:1, 15; Isaiah 44:3; Ezekiel 39:29;*
*Joel 2:28-29; Zechariah 12:10;*
*Acts 2:5-6; 38; 10:45; Romans 5:5*

Do we envy the Old Testament prophets upon whom God poured out his Spirit? Most of what they said and wrote were warnings and promises that things will get better some day. But they had to wait for visions or movement of the Spirit so they could write what we have in writing today.

Now we have it all! How? We don't have to wait for a vision or movement of the Spirit. And we can read their writings any time we want! Not only that, but we understand what they wrote better than the prophets who wrote them.

Peter explains it dynamically: "Of this salvation the prophets have inquired and searched carefully, who prophesied of the grace that would come to you, searching what, or what manner of time, the Spirit of Christ who was in them was indicating when he testified beforehand the sufferings of Christ and the glories that would follow. To them it was revealed that, not to themselves, but to us they were ministering the things which now have been reported to you through those who have preached the gospel to you by the Holy Spirit sent from heaven ~ things which angels desire to look into" (I Peter 1:10-12).

Paul shows another way we are blessed today. "Now hope does not disappoint because the love of God has been **poured** out in our hearts by the Holy Spirit [Word of God] who was given to us" (Romans 5:5).

## POWER & MIGHT

*Romans 15:13; Romans 1:4; I Corinthians 15:42-46; Ephesians 6:12; I Thessalonians 1:5; II Timothy 1:7; Hebrews 6:4-5*

Romans 15:13 adds power to our hope: "Now may the God of hope fill you with all joy and peace in believing that you may be abounding hope by the **power** of the Holy Spirit." He further proclaims, "God has not given us a spirit of fear, but of **power** and of love and of a sound mind" (II Timothy 1:7).

Everyone wants to go to heaven, but seldom does anyone want to die. We Christians need not fear death. I Corinthians 15:42-46 says that our body is "sown in corruption" but raised in incorruption. "It is sown in weakness, it is raised in **power**. It is sown a natural body, it is raised a spiritual body."

## SPEAKING & PROPHECY

*I Corinthians 12:3; Ephesians 5:18-19; I John 4:1-3; Revelation 19:10b*

When we tell someone we believe Jesus is the Son of God, that is the Spirit within us **speaking** (I Corinthians 12:3). Whenever we speak of Jesus, that is the Spirit of **prophecy**.

When we don't **speak** it, we sing it (Ephesians 5:18-19). We can't hold back. Have you ever sung hymns around the house or in the car? You just can't hold it back.

We have the advantage over people who lived during Bible times, for we have all the prophecies God wanted us to have written down. II Peter 1:20-21 explains that **prophecy** is scripture. So, if someone claims to be prophesying today, if it is different than the scripture, it must be challenged. Or does God continue to give scriptures to some people, but not let the rest of us know what it is?

# GIFTS/GIVEN

*Acts 2:38; Acts 5:32; Romans 5:5; Romans 12:6-8, 11;*
*I Corinthians 2:12-14; II Corinthians 3:6;*
*II Corinthians 5:2-5; I John 4:13*

We have been through the special spiritual gifts of people in New Testament times before the New Testament was written. We have also learned in I Corinthians 13 that these gifts were to cease. Are we left without any gifts? Not at all.

Romans 12:6-8 lists gifts that are available to all Christians, then and now

**Prophecy** ~ in the sense of sharing the scriptures with others

**Ministering** to others ~ helping the sick, or the tired mother, or the orphaned child, the bereaved, the hungry, etc.

**Teaching** ~ home studies, formal Bible studies, small informal groups, individuals

**Exhorting** ~ those who have fallen away to come back to the church, those who are weighed down with problems, those who are new Christians, etc.

**Giving** ~ by those who have a talent for earning money and desire to help others with it

**Leading** ~ in such a way that people will want to follow

**Merciful** ~ toward those who have fallen in sin

We do not need miraculous gifts to be of service in the kingdom of God. Instead of performing miracles to prove the Bible is divine, we can prove we believe it and be an example to others.

# FILLED

*Romans 15:13; Ephesians 5:18-19*

Paul exhorted the church in Ephesus (western seaport in today's Turkey), "Do not be drunk with wine, in which is dissipation; but be **filled** with the Spirit, speaking to one another in psalms, hymns and spiritual songs, singing and making melody in your heart to the Lord" (Ephesians 5:18-19). There was a Christian family in Corinth in today's Greece who had "addicted themselves to the ministry of the saints" (II Corinthians 16:15 KJV).

How can we be thus addicted? Adapting the Mayo Clinic signs of addiction, let us apply it to our Christian life:

1. Feeling we have to pray regularly, several times a day.
2. Failing in our attempts to stop singing about the love of Jesus.
3. Making certain we maintain a supply of Bible and other Christian study materials.
4. Spending money when we cannot afford it on Christian benevolence.
5. Doing things we normally wouldn't do to obtain more Bible knowledge, such as quitting a club taking up too much time.
6. Feeling that, to deal with problems, we need God.
7. Doing risky activities when we are under the influence of God, such as telling our friends about Jesus.
8. Focusing more and more time and energy on getting and using prayer.

We are blessed when we read Paul's prayer for the church in Rome, and for the church everywhere and in all eras: "Now may the God of hope **fill** you with all joy and peace in believing, that you may abound in hope by the power of the Holy Spirit" (Romans 15:13).

# 12. Relationship With Believers
# After the New Testament
# Was Written-II

## REVIEW

Jesus was what? John 1:1 and 14 says he was the Word of God that we could see for awhile. The Holy Spirit is what? John 14:17 and 17:17 says he is the Word of God that we can read.

This is the most tangible evidence we have of God's Holy Spirit. We don't have to guess. We have the Word of God in its entirety that we can read any time we want.

## SEAL/DEPOSIT/PROMISE/GUARANTEE

*Acts 1:4-5; 2:1-4; Acts 2:32-33; Romans 1:1-4;*
*II Corinthians 1:21-22; II Corinthians 5:2-5; Galatians 3:13-14;*
*Ephesians 1:13-14; Ephesians 3:4-6; Ephesians 4:30-31;*
*II Timothy 1:13-14*

We are not talking here about a seal such as is used on legal papers to verify someone's position such as a notary public, or on a diploma to verify the university president's signature, or etc. This seal is not a thing. It is an action. But, in both cases, both kinds of seals, it is a verification.

We are sealed with the guarantee of our salvation. Ephesians 1:13-14 explains, "In him you also trusted after you heard the word of truth, the gospel of your salvation; in whom also, having believed, you were **sealed** with the Holy Spirit of Promise, who is the **guarantee** of our inheritance until the redemption of the purchased possession, to the praise of his glory." We see here that our seal is our promise, our guarantee that God will keep his promise.

II Corinthians 5:2-5 says God "has given us the Spirit as a **guarantee** of our salvation." How can the Holy Spirit be our

70

guarantee? Because, remember, the Holy Spirit is the Word of God (John 14:17 and 17:17). We know we have the guarantee because the Bible says so.

Well, how do we know the Bible is true? Regarding the Old Testament, there were numerous prophecies in it of world kingdoms at their height that they would collapse some day, it happened just as God said it would. No man could have known those things ahead of time. And how do we know the New Testament is true? Because of the numerous prophecies of the coming world Savior and King made in the Old Testament that were fulfilled in Jesus in the New Testament.

"Now he who establishes us with you in Christ and has anointed us is God who also has **sealed** us and given us the Spirit in our hearts as a **guarantee**" (II Corinthians 1:21-22). Who is the us? It is Paul, the writer, and all the Christians in Corinth. God only anoints us to be two things: Kings and priests. All Jews knew from the Old Testament that the only ones who were anointed were kings (to make them kings) and priests (to make them priests). So, what does anointing do for a Christian? It isn't a special "calling" to do a particular thing. It is to make us priests and kings. All Christians are that right now.

Revelation spells it out in 5:10: "And have redeemed us to God by your blood out of every tribe and tongue and people and nation, and have made us kings and priests to our God; and we shall reign on the earth." Yes, we Christians are reigning on the earth right now!

## PRAYER/WORSHIP

*John 4:23-24; Acts 13:2-4; Romans 8:23, 26-27; Romans 15:30; Ephesians 1:16-18; Philippians 1:13-21; Philippians 3:3; Jude 1:20-21*

Paul was a huge believer in prayer. He even begged for it in Romans 15:30, "I beg you, brethren, through the Lord Jesus Christ, and through the love of the Spirit, that you strive together with me in **prayers** to God for me."

The brother of Jesus, Jude, said in verses 20 and 21, "But you, beloved, building yourselves up on your most holy faith, **praying** in the Holy Spirit, keep yourselves in the love of God, looking for the mercy of our Lord Jesus Christ unto eternal life."

In Romans 8:23, 26, 27, we learn that the Holy Spirit helps us in our **prayers** when we are so deep in desire and thought that we cannot express it. The Bible calls it "groanings." This is from the Greek word *stenazo* meaning to sigh.

When Jesus healed someone who could not speak or hear, he groaned, he sighed (Mark 7:34). When the Israelites were crying out to God because of their slavery, they groaned, they sighed (Acts 7:34). We Christians long to be released from this hard life so we can rest in Jesus in heaven. "For in this we groan, earnestly desiring to be clothed with our habitation which is from heaven....that mortality may be swallowed up by life" (see II Corinthians 5:2-5).

Who do we groan for? Only ourselves? That is selfish. That will come when we groan for others. Groaning is hard to do. It is hard on us mentally. But do we kneel in prayer with our congregation's membership directory before us, and groan for every member of our congregation? Do we kneel in prayer with our newspaper before us, and groan for all those people experiencing tragedies or trying to develop a cause, or getting married?

God is just waiting for us to ask. "Therefore, the Lord will wait, that he may be gracious to you; and therefore he will be exalted that he may have mercy on you" (Isaiah 30:18).

# PEACE/COMFORT

*John 14:16-17; John 14:26-27; John 15:26; John 16:7;*
*Acts 9:1, 18, 31; Romans 8:5-6; Romans 14:17-18; Romans 15:13;*
*Galatians 5:22-23; Ephesians 4:2-6; Philippians 1:1-2;*
*Revelation 1:4*

Amidst this world of turmoil, are we ever able to live in peace? In John 12:31 and 14:30, Jesus calls Satan the ruler of this world, or sometimes translated the prince of this world. Paul calls him the god of this age. This world was never intended to be our home. Heaven is our home. We are just on the proving ground, on the road to whatever destination we choose. Is there turmoil in our work, in our family, in our government? How do we escape the turmoil?

"The kingdom of God is not eating and drinking, but righteousness and **peace** and joy in the Holy Spirit" (Romans 14:17). "The fruit of the Spirit is love, joy, **peace**, longsuffering, kindness, goodness, faithfulness, gentleness, self-control. Against such there is no law" (Galatians 5:22-23).

So how do we find peace amidst the turmoil? By making time to do good things for others. By showing gentleness when there is arguing and bickering. By being right in our own behavior amidst people and governments who are not. By telling ourselves to be patient, for God is at work, and he is ultimately in control.

How does our congregation get along? Is it overall consumed with complaining? Or is there peace?

Paul spelled out congregational problems several times in II Timothy where he said people are led astray by people with large egos who claim to be doing things for the sake of the church, but they are fooling themselves and actually doing it to get their own way. We must ask ourselves when we are arguing for or against a program of the church, "If I moved away, would this congregation survive without me?". The answer is obvious. Of course, it would.

"...with all lowliness and gentleness, with longsuffering bearing with one another in love, endeavoring to keep the unity of the Spirit in the bond of **peace**. There is one body and one Spirit, just as you were called in one hope of your calling: One Lord, one faith, one baptism; one God and Father of all, who is above all, and through all, and in you all" (Ephesians 4:2-6).

# FELLOWSHIP/COMMUNION/LOVE

*John 14:15-17; Romans 15:30; II Corinthians 6:4, 6;*
*II Corinthians 13:14; Galatians 5:22-23;*

*Philippians 2:1-2*

Here, we say with Paul, "The grace of the Lord Jesus Christ, and the love of God, and the **communion** of the Holy Spirit be with you all" (II Corinthians 13:14). "If there be any **fellowship** of the Spirit, if any affection and mercy, fulfill my joy by being likeminded, having the same love, being of one accord" (Philippians 2:2).

Yes, indeed, we can have fellowship with the Holy Spirit. It is not a momentary thing. It is an all-the-time thing. The entire 139th Psalm reveals it wondrously.

O LORD, You have searched me and known *me*.
² You know my sitting down and my rising up;
You understand my thought afar off.
³ You comprehend my path and my lying down,
And are acquainted with all my ways.
⁴ For *there is* not a word on my tongue,
*But* behold, O LORD, You know it altogether.
⁵ You have hedged me behind and before,
And laid Your hand upon me.
⁶ *Such* knowledge *is* too wonderful for me;
It is high, I cannot *attain* it.
⁷ Where can I go from Your Spirit?
Or where can I flee from Your presence?
⁸ If I ascend into heaven, You *are* there;
If I make my bed in hell, behold, You *are there*.
⁹ *If* I take the wings of the morning,
*And* dwell in the uttermost parts of the sea,
¹⁰ Even there Your hand shall lead me,
And Your right hand shall hold me.
¹¹ If I say, "Surely the darkness shall fall[a] on me,"
Even the night shall be light about me;
¹² Indeed, the darkness shall not hide from You,
But the night shines as the day;
The darkness and the light *are* both alike *to You*.
¹³ For You formed my inward parts;

You covered me in my mother's womb.
14 I will praise You, for I am fearfully *and* wonderfully made;[b]
Marvelous are Your works,
And *that* my soul knows very well.
15 My frame was not hidden from You,
When I was made in secret,
*And* skillfully wrought in the lowest parts of the earth.
16 Your eyes saw my substance, being yet unformed.
And in Your book they all were written,
The days fashioned for me,
When *as yet there were* none of them.
17 How precious also are Your thoughts to me, O God!
How great is the sum of them!
18 *If* I should count them,
they would be more in number than the sand;
When I awake, I am still with You.
19 Oh, that You would slay the wicked, O God!
Depart from me, therefore, you bloodthirsty men.
20 For they speak against You wickedly;
Your enemies take *Your name* in vain.[c]
21 Do I not hate them, O LORD, who hate You?
And do I not loathe those who rise up against You?
22 I hate them with perfect hatred;
I count them my enemies.
23 Search me, O God, and know my heart;
Try me, and know my anxieties;
24 And see if *there is any* wicked way in me,
And lead me in the way everlasting.

How do we know God's Holy Spirit is in us? When someone dies, we say that person's spirit has left him. Was that person consciously aware of his spirit while he was alive? No. He just knew because of the evidence: He was still walking around, talking, communicating with others, doing, acting. It is the same with the Holy Spirit within us.

J. W. McGarvey (1829-1911) said, "The fact of this indwelling is not a matter of consciousness; for consciousness is limited in its operation to the cognition of the mind's own states and actions....Neither is the fact that I have a human spirit dwelling in me a matter of consciousness. I know the latter, as I know the former, only by faith....Revelation teaches me to look for certain fruit of the Spirit by which I know that the Holy Spirit dwells in me. When I find love, joy, peace, long-suffering, kindness, goodness, faithfulness and temperance characterizing my life, I know the Spirit of God dwells in me....

"I must cooperate with the Holy Spirit by an active exertion of my own will in the direction of love, joy, peace, etc., and that, when I enjoy these blessed frames of mind, I am enjoying them in fellowship with the Holy Spirit....They are not his fruit alone, nor mine alone, but they are partly mine and partly his, so that he and I have fellowship in them....boldly pray, then, not only for the grace of Christ and the love of God but also for the fellowship of the Holy Spirit."

# JOY/REJOICE

*Psalm 51:10-15; Luke 10:21; Acts 13:49-52; Acts 15:3, 8;*
*Romans 14:17-18; Romans 15:13-14; Galatians 5:22-23;*
*I Thessalonians 1:6-8*

Being forgiven of our sins brings joy. David said, "Create in me a clean heart, O God, and renew a steadfast spirit within me. Do not cast me away from your presence, and do not take your Holy Spirit from me. Restore to me the **joy** of your salvation, and uphold me by your generous Spirit" (Psalm 51:10-15).

Death can bring joy. Not to the world, but to Christians. To the world, there is darkness, a valley of shadows and death (Psalm 23). But to the Christian, light has sprung up in the valley of the shadow of death (Luke 1:78, 79; Matthew 4:16).

Even persecution can bring joy. The church in Thessalonica in northern Greece suffered much persecution. But Paul wrote them, "You became followers of us and of the Lord, having received the

Word in much affliction, with **joy** of the Holy Spirit" (I Thessalonians 1:6-8). Jesus said in the Sermon on the Mount, "Blessed **[happy]** are those who are persecuted for righteousness' sake, for theirs is the kingdom of heaven" (Matthew 5:10).

Jesus forewarned his followers that they would be persecuted (John 15:20), so after his apostles were flogged, they **rejoiced** that they had been counted worthy to be persecuted (Acts 5:40-42).

II Timothy 3:12 says that all who live godly will be persecuted. Have we ever been persecuted for sharing the gospel? Did we go back for more? Just how godly are we? Through the pain, can we rejoice? Can we have deep-down joy in the Holy Spirit? Indeed, we can!

# 13. Relationship With the Whole World ~ I

## DEATH

*Romans 1:2-4; Roans 6:4-5; Romans 7:12-15; Romans 8:1-7; Romans 8:11, 13; I Corinthians15:42-46; II Corinthians 3:7-11; Philippians 1:17-21; Hebrews 9:14; I Peter 3:18; Revelation 1:4-5; Revelation 14:13*

### Physical

There was no death in the world until someone sinned. Remember, death literally means separation.

We do not know how long Adam and Eve lived blissfully in the Garden of Eden. Perhaps ten years, perhaps a hundred years. Adam was 130 years old when Seth was born (Genesis 5:3). Seth was born after their oldest son Cain and second son Abel, were born. In fact, Seth was born after Cain killed Abel (Genesis 5:25).

The way the Genesis account reads, Cain was born after they left the Garden of Eden because Eve's punishment was that she would bring forth children in pain (Genesis 3:16). So it is doubtful they lived in the Garden more than a hundred years.

Sin was introduced in the Garden of Eden, but physical death did not occur for another few centuries when Adam was 930 years old (Genesis 5:4) He had a lot of time to think about the consequences of his sin.

God told Adam after he sinned with Eve that he would have to work hard for his food from then on. Further, he was destined to "return to the ground, for out of it you were taken; for dust you are, and to dust you shall return".

What a reminder! These bodies we value so much, these bodies we spend time and money on are just chunks of clay, and not very valuable clay at that. The human body is made up of 65% oxygen, 18% carbon, 10% hydrogen, 3% nitrogen, 1.5% calcium, 1% phosphorous, .25% potassium, .25% sulfur, .15% sodium, .15%

chlorine, .05% magnesium, .0004% iron, and .00004% iodine. What is the going rate for the elements in the human body? About one US dollar!

Jesus brought three people back to life to show his power over life and death. He brought back the widow's son in Nain (Luke 7:12-15), Jairus' daughter (Matthew 9:18-26), and Lazarus (John 11). We can only imagine the emotional grief that consumed families of the boy, the girl, and the man.

When Jesus went to Lazarus' grave, he groaned in his Spirit. The word "groan" in Greek is *embri-mao-mai*, which is intense anger like the snorting of horses. God's Spirit, who is Life, and Jesus who is Life, were angry at death. Maybe Jesus clenched his fists and gritted his teeth, and silently announced to Satan, "We're going to have it out here and now!"

Jesus cried with a loud voice. It wasn't just loud so Lazarus could hear. It was a threat. In Greek, it was *kraugazo*, a bellow, a roar. This same word was used when the mob demanded that Jesus be crucified (John 18:40). Jesus was angry at physical death. He was even more angry at spiritual death.

By understanding the emotional and physical pain of body death, it helps us understand spiritual death.

## Spiritual

God told Adam he could eat anything in the garden he wanted except for the Tree of the Knowledge of Good and Evil. He warned him that the day he ate of it, he would die (Genesis 2:16-17). Eve was created after God's warning. How many times did Adam explain it to Eve? It was to him God gave the order. When Eve finally gave in and ate it, Adam was nearby and apparently did not try to stop her. She ate it, then gave some to Adam "who was with her." Perhaps he wanted to see if she would keel over when she ate. When she didn't, perhaps he thought he was safe and that God had either lied to them (Satan's version of the warning), or they had outsmarted God (Satan's version of God's motives) and become as clever as him.

But it happened just as God had warned. The moment they ate of the fruit, their souls died. Maybe they didn't realize it until later when God called them. But as soon as they had to face God, they hid (Genesis 3:910). The souls of Adam and Eve became separated from God. Their souls had died. The same thing will happen at the end of the world when God calls all mankind.

"The sky receded as a scroll…and the kings of the earth, the great man, the rich men, the commanders, the mighty men, every slave and every free man hid themselves in the caves and in the rocks of the mountains and said to the mountains and rocks, 'Fall on us and hide us from the face of him who sits on the throne and from the wrath of the Lamb! For the great day of is wrath has come, and who is able to stand?' " (Revelation 6:14-17).

God is sinless and cannot coexist with sin. It is like light co-existing with darkness; it is impossible. So it is with God; he cannot co-exist with sin. If he did, he would be condoning sin and no longer exist. That, too, is impossible.

# SIN/TRANSGRESSION/INIQUITY/ REBELLION

*Isaiah 30:1; Isaiah 59:18-21; Hosea 9:7; Micah 3:8; Matthew 12:31-33; John 20:20-23; Acts 2:38; Romans 8:1-9, 13; I Corinthians 6:16-20; Galatians 5:16-21; Galatians 6:1; Hebrews 3:7-8; Hebrews 10:26, 29; I Peter 3:18; Revelation 1:4-5*

There is a great warfare going on out there ~ good versus evil. Satan wants to be our god. He has been a liar and murderer since the beginning (John 8:44). He doesn't want to go to hell alone, so he tells us our sins are fun. Isaiah warned in 5:20, "Woe to those who call evil good, and good evil; who put darkness for light, and light for darkness; who put bitter for sweet, and sweet for bitter."

There are 788 verses in the Bible on sin (yes, I counted them). Plus, there are innumerable verses that say, "Do not do this," or "Do that" which don't use the word sin. Plus, there are passages regarding people sinning by example. In all this, Satan lies to people and says everyone is going to heaven when they die, though Satan knows this is not true. He is successful in feeding this lie to people because it is a popular lie.

## Definitions

There are two different words used in the Bible to describe sin.

The first definition is to trespass or go where we're not supposed to go. In Hebrew it is *pasha*, and in Greek it is *hamartema*. This kind of sin is bad committed.

Micah said in 3:8, "But truly I am full of power by the Spirit of the Lord, and of justice and might, to declare to Jacob his **transgression**, and to Israel his sin."

NO
TRESPASSING

THIS PROPERTY
IS PROTECTED BY
VIDEO SURVEILLANCE

TRESPASSERS WILL
BE PROSECUTED

The second definition is to fall short of the target. In Hebrew it is *chata,* and in Greek it is *hamartano.* This kind of sin is good omitted.

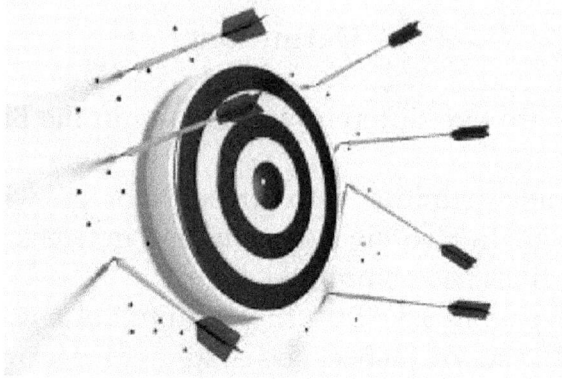

"For Christ also suffered once for sins, the just for the unjust, that he might bring us to God, being put to death in the flesh but made alive by the Spirit" (I Peter 3:18).

There are fourteen lists of sins just in the New Testament. There are nineteen statements or lists of things we are not to do which are not called sin, but obviously are sin (murder, committing adultery, getting drunk, etc.). There are ten statements or lists of good things that, if omitted, are sin.

In every case, when we commit sin, according to Ephesians 4:25-31, we grieve the Holy Spirit. Further, Hebrews 10:29 says that, when we sin, we trample underfoot the Son of God and insult the Spirit of Grace.

## BODY/FLESH & BLOOD

*Acts 2:31-33; Romans 6:4-5; Romans 8:3-4, 13;*
*I Corinthians 16:16-20; I Corinthians 10:3-5; I Corinthians 12:13;*
*I Corinthians 15:42-46; Ephesians 3:4-6; Ephesians 4:4-9;*
*Ephesians 6:12; I Timothy 3:16; I Peter 3:18; I John 5:6-8*

We are not a body with a mind and soul. We are a mind and

soul with a body. We need our body to get our mind around. We have different vehicles (types of bodies) for our minds to get around in.

Hebrews 9 and 10 talks about the arrangement of the tabernacle with the two different rooms and furnishings. If the Jews, under the direction of Moses, had not built it like God said to, we wouldn't have understood the spiritual version of the tabernacle.

Hebrews 9:13-14 refers to animal sacrifices on the altar in the tabernacle, and that Jesus has become that sacrifice. Verse 12 says the Holy of Holies (Most Holy Place) in the tabernacle is now heaven. Verse 11 says the high priest now entering the Holy of Holies is Jesus. Hebrews 10:20 even says regarding the curtain that blocked the Holy of Holies from anyone but the High Priest entering it, was now Jesus who opens and invites everyone in.

Our body also helps us understand spiritual things. I Corinthians 6:19 explains that our bodies are the temple of the Holy Spirit. So, what do we use our bodies for? Where do we take our mind, our soul, the Holy Spirit with our bodies?

Further, why did Jesus have to come in a body? Why did the Word of God (John 1:1, 14) have to come in a body?

Remember, sin is going into territory we should not be in, and it is missing the target of perfection. God told Adam that the day he sinned, his soul would die. Romans 3:23 says everyone sins, and 6:23 says the wages of sin is death ~ what we earn when we sin. This is a spiritual law that cannot be broken. God cannot co-exist with sin; if he did, he would go out of existence. Since God is life, it is impossible for him to go out of existence. So, the death penalty has to be paid.

Because it is impossible for us to not sin, and since Satan is the prince of this world, in God's love he provided a temporary fix. He said we could kill animals in our place when we sinned (see Exodus 12). Then, once a year, the Jewish High Priest could kill a bull and goat for all the Jews at one time, and sprinkle the animals' blood in the temple. This was called the Day of Atonement" (see Leviticus 16). Both the body dying and the blood being shed were important.

Always the substitute animals had to be completely without blemish. They couldn't be blind, injured, maimed, have warts, or anything else (see Leviticus 4). Even then, these were only temporary fixes because it is not possible for the blood of bulls and goats to take away sin (Hebrews 10:3-4).

So Jesus, the Word of God, entered the body of a human so he could be perfect without moral blemish (II Corinthians 5:21; Hebrews 4:15), and be the final substitute (Colossians 2:9-10; Hebrews 10:5). He was called the perfect Lamb of God (John 1:29; I Peter 1:19).

Further, Jesus had to have a body with blood (Romans 5:6-9; Ephesians 1:7). The blood of Jesus was to purify us from all our sins (I John 1:7). He paid our death penalty in full, thus purchasing the freedom of all nations throughout the world (Revelation 5:9) if they would believe he did all this.

On the cross, Jesus did away with the old Law of Moses completely with its over 600 laws including animal sacrifices, burning candles and incense in worship, having a separate priesthood, stoning for adultery, etc. (Colossians 2:14). He took the blame for every filthy sin committed by every person since the beginning of the world (I Peter 2:22-24). He died spiritually on the cross when he cried out that God had forsaken him (Mark 15:34), for he was now completely separated from God. Then he suffered separation from this world when he died physically (John 19:40).

That, my dear reader, is why sin grieves the Holy Spirit.

## COMMAND

*Matthew 28:19-20; John 14:15-18; Romans 2:25, 29; Romans 8:6-8; I Corinthians 14:37; I John 3:24*

The world doesn't think God cares what they do. We commit all kinds of trespasses, knowing there is 24-hour surveillance from heaven; but we convince ourselves not to think about it. Still, we claim "I am a Christian." Are we? Acts 11:26 says Christians are disciples. And Jesus said in John 8:31 that we are his disciples only if we keep his **commandments.**

When Balaam prophesied in favor of the Israelites about to invade their land, Balaam said, "I could not go beyond the Word of the Lord" (Numbers 24:13). Joshua was full of the spirit of wisdom and based his own leadership of the Israelites on what the Lord had **commanded** Moses (Deuteronomy 34:9).

Instead, we fool ourselves, we put blinders on in order to claim we are Christians. Owning a Bible does not automatically make us a Christian any more than owning a scout handbook just automatically makes us a scout. Showing up at church services does not automatically make us a Christian any more than showing up at scout meetings just automatically makes us a scout. Memorizing verses in the Bible does not automatically make us a Christian any more than memorizing the scout oath just automatically makes us a scout. Even living in a nation of Christians does not automatically make us a Christian any more than living in a nation with scouts in it just automatically makes us a scout. Being a Christian is just not automatic.

If we don't read the Bible for ourselves, we cannot know his commandments. We must not rely on religious leaders because too many of them contradict each other. We must read the Bible for ourselves. More specifically, we must read the New Testament of the Bible for ourselves and quit hiding our head in the sand. The New Testament is only about 300 pages long, the size of the average novel. It is not impossible.

The apostle John said in I John 3:24, "Now he who keeps his **commandments** abides in him, and he in him. And by this we know that he abides in us, by the Spirit whom he has given us."

# 14. Relationship With the Whole World ~ II

## TESTING/TRYING

*Acts 5:3-9; Hebrews 3:7-8; I John 4:1-2*

Should we test the Spirit of God? Only if we are looking among other religions to discover which is the true God. In that case, we are actually testing the spirit of the other religions. We are not to test is Spirit once we discover who the true God is.

But a lot of people test him anyway as though all the things he said he didn't really mean. God warned Cain, "sin lies at the door," but he killed Abel anyway. The result? He was exiled the rest of his life. (See Genesis 4:1-15.)

Noah warned people for a hundred years to leave their sin because God said his Spirit was not going to **strive** with them forever, and they saw how convinced he was because they saw his boat; but they stuck to all the fun of their sins anyway. The result? They were drowned in the flood. (See Genesis 6).

Nadab and Abihu were told to take the fire for their sacrifices and incense from one particular source, but they did it their way (a more convenient way?) and took it from a different source anyway. The result? They were burned by their unauthorized fire (Leviticus 10:1-3).

The Jews, recently freed from slavery by the only true God, went out into the desert and worshiped a calf anyway. The result? Thousands died. (See Exodus 32.) Over and over they rebelled against the one who was only trying to save them. Hebrews 3:7-8 recalls, "Therefore, as the Holy Spirit says, 'Today, if you will hear his voice, do not harden your hearts as in the rebellion in the days of **trial** in the wilderness."

Over and over in the book of Judges, the Israelites worshiped God awhile, then began worshiping idols and doing other things that pleased only themselves and not God. The result? Every few years when they did that, God would hand them over to foreigners to rule them.

Ananias and Sapphira told one little lie to make themselves look better than they really were. Peter demanded to know, "How is it that you have agreed together to **test** the Spirit of the Lord?". The result? They died immediately.

Once we know and acknowledge who God is, why do we keep testing him to see if he meant what he said?

Both Isaiah and Jeremiah tried mightily to stop this type of behavior before people destroyed themselves in the midst of all their fun.

"But they **rebelled** and grieved his Holy Spirit. So he turned himself against them as an enemy, and he fought against them" (Isaiah 63:10).

"Woe to those who call evil good, and good evil" (Isaiah 5:20-23).

"They have lied about the Lord and said, 'It is not he, neither will evil come upon us" (Jeremiah 5:12-13).

"The word of the Lord is offensive to them" (Jeremiah 6:10b, 17).

"Will you steal, murder, commit adultery and then....say, 'We are safe'?" (Jeremiah 7:9, 10-NIV).

"....No man repented of his wickedness, saying, 'What have I done?' " (Jeremiah 8:5-6).

"...They have taught their tongue to speak lies; they weary themselves to commit iniquity" (Jeremiah 9:5).

God is not trying to keep us from having fun. He is trying to keep us out of hell! Once again we return to one of the prophets who begged his people to stop their sins.

*'Return, backsliding___' says the Lord;*
*'I will not cause my anger to fall on you.*
*For I am merciful,' says the Lord.*
*Jeremiah 3:12b*

*Your iniquities have turned these things away,*

87

*And your sins have withheld good from you.*
*Jeremiah 5:25*

*Are they not rather harming themselves?*
*Jeremiah 7:19b [NIV]*

*'For I know the plans I have for you!'*
*declares the Lord,*
*'plans to prosper you and not to harm you,*
*plans to give you hope and a future.'*
*Jeremiah 29:11*

God's Spirit longs to change the hearts of those who do not love him. What does he do?

Psalm 51:10 – Creates a clean heart
Psalm 143:4 – Relieves a distressed heart
Isaiah 61:1 – Heals the brokenhearted
Ezekiel 11:19 – Takes away a heart of stone and replaces it with a soft heart
Ezekiel 18:31 – Gives a new heart that will not die
Romans 2:29 – Cuts sin off people's heart
Romans 5:5 – Gives people hope
Romans 8:27 – Helps people understand his will (the Bible)
II Corinthians 1:22 – Helps people believe in heaven and hell, God and Satan
Galatians 4:4-7 – Helps people believe they can be adopted children of God

We must test various religions. Which is the true God? Once we select our religion, we must test it (not God, but the religion).

The apostle John warned after the church had been in existence for several decades, "Beloved, do not believe every spirit, but **test** the spirits, whether they are of God; because many false prophets have gone out into the world" (I John 4:1).

Are there leaders who act "holier than thou" (Isaiah 65:5)?

Who are greedy, so practice deceit to get a bigger paycheck (Jeremiah 8:10)? Who speak visions from their own minds (Jeremiah 23:16)?

What about the worship services? We know Jesus nailed the old Law of Moses to the cross (Galatians 2:14). But do we know enough about the Law of Moses to tell if we are dipping into that old law for our Christian worship and organization? Like a separate priesthood? Or burning incense and candles? Tithing? Playing on instruments? If we dip into these things, we must do them all. That includes a high priest, paid choirs and orchestras performing daily at the church building, animal sacrifices, ceremonial circumcisions, and even stoning for adultery. If we do part of the law, we must keep it all (James 2:10; Galatians 5:3).

Jesus said, "If you love me, you will keep my commandments" (John 14:15). The leaders of all religions throughout the world will be judged some day along with the rest of us.

# BELIEF/FAITH

*John 7:38-39; Acts 6:3, 5; Acts 10:44-46; Acts 11:22-24;*
*Acts 13:8-10; Acts 14:7-9; I Corinthians 12:9; Galatians 3:12; Galatians*
*3:5-8, 14; Ephesians 1:13; Ephesians 4:4-6;*
*II Thessalonians 2:13; I Timothy 3:16; I Timothy 4:1-2; I John 4:1-2; I*
*John 4:13 – 14; Jude 1:19-20*

Faith in what? Hebrews 11:1 says **faith** has evidence. How do we choose a religion? We can read the "holy" books of world religions to see if we chose right when we chose Christianity. Do those other books have built-in proofs they are really from God? We must decide which book to believe in.

Paul said, "O foolish Galatians! Who has bewitched you that you should not obey the truth, before whose eyes Jesus Christ was clearly portrayed among you as crucified? This only I want to learn from you: Did you receive the Spirit by the works of the law or by the hearing of **faith**?" (Galatians 3:1-2). The Bible is the only such book in existence that has those built-in proofs through prophecies fulfilled (entire nations, and a promised Savior). And today we have the proofs of archaeology, history, and ancient manuscripts.

We must not only believe the Bible is divine, but we must also believe Jesus is divine. How do we know for sure? Once we decide the Bible is true, we look for other evidences (Hebrews 11:1). We have proofs he died because his close friend, Judas, identified him. The crowd recognized him. The Sanhedrin tried him. The Roman governor condemned him. The soldiers nailed him to the cross and guarded him until he died. We have proofs he came back to life because both the Sanhedrin and Roman governor sealed and placed guards at the tomb, but his body disappeared anyway. They were never able to produce his body. Jesus appeared to over 500 people alive again. The Sanhedrin never did produce his body when confronting his apostles.

What else must we believe? We must believe in Satan and hell ~ Satan so we can fight him, and hell so we can do everything possible to avoid it and find safety in the Savior (Saving One). And we must believe we sin. Hell has already been discussed in this study, and so has sin. Go back and look at those chapters. Do we all believe we sin and deserve our wages of hell? Do we all believe Jesus being in our lives daily is the only way to heaven? Jesus said, " 'He who **believes** in me, as the Scripture has said, out of his heart will flow rivers of living water.' By this he spoke concerning the Spirit whom those **believing** in him would receive; for the Holy Sprit was not yet given because Jesus was not yet glorified" (John 7:38-39). So, we must believe in Jesus.

The word "faith" in the Greek is *pistis*, meaning faithfulness, steadfastness, commitment. Paul said, "In him you also trusted, after you heard the word of truth, the gospel of your salvation; in who also, having **believed**, you were sealed with the Holy Spirit of promise" (Ephesians 1:13).

# HEART

*Genesis 6:3-6; Psalm 51:10-17; Psalm 143:4, 7, 10;*

*Proverbs 1:20-23; Isaiah 61:1; Ezekiel 11:18-19; Ezekiel 18:31; Ezekiel*
*36:26-27; Zechariah 7:11-12; Mark 2:8; Acts 5:1-5;*
*Acts 7:51, 53; Acts 15:8-9; Acts 28:17, 25-27; Romans 2:25, 29;*
*Romans 5:5; Romans 8:27; II Corinthians 1::22; II Corinthians 3:3;*
*Galatians 4:4-7; Ephesians 5:18-19; Colossians 3:16; Hebrews 3:7-8;*
*Hebrews 4:12-13*

We can resist the Holy Spirit. God said in Genesis 6:3-6 that his Spirit was not always going to strive with man; then he sent the flood. Zechariah 7:11-12 said people made their **hearts** like flint, refusing to listen to the Word of God sent by his Spirit. Satan filled the **heart** of Ananias and Sapphire to lie about their contribution so they would look better before others (Acts 5:1-5).

But many beautiful scriptures explain what the Holy Spirit does for our heart. David said in Psalm 51:10, "Create in me a clean **heart** O God, and renew a steadfast spirit within me. Do not cast me away from your presence, and do not take your Holy Spirit from me" (Psalm 51:10-11). Isaiah 61:1 predicts Jesus when he said, "The Spirit of the Lord God is upon me because the Lord has anointed me to preach good tidings to the poor; he has sent me to heal the **brokenhearted**" (Isaiah 61:1).

Ezekiel said God will put a new spirit within us, take away the stony heart and give us a soft **heart**" (Ezekiel 11:18-19). Most beautiful is what Paul expressed: "Now hope does not disappoint, because the love of God has been poured out in our **hearts** by the Holy Spirit who was given to us" (Romans 5:5).

## OBEYING/KEEPING

*II Chronicles 24:20-21; Matthew 28:18-20; John 14:15-17, 21; Acts*
*5:32; Romans 15:18-19; Galatians 5:5, 7-10; I John 3:24*

Only when we obey the Word of God (the Holy Spirit) will any of our knowledge do us any good. We can be scholars of the Bible and not obey it. We must believe with our head, our heart, and our life. It must be life changing. Difficult to do? A lot of the time it is. But not impossible. And God's Holy Spirit helps us want to obey if we don't fight him.

Paul warned, "For we through the Spirit eagerly wait for the hope of righteousness by faith....Who hindered you from **obeying the truth?**" (Galatians 5:5, 7). Lest we think we have God's protection against hell, we must remind ourselves that only those who keep his commandments abide in him and are given the Holy Spirit to protect them (I John 3:24 and Acts 5:32).

How much should we obey? All of it. Jesus said, "If you love me, **keep** my commandments. And I will pray the Father, and he will give you another Helper that he may abide with you forever ~ the Spirit of Truth (John 14:15-17).

If the world only would stop its constant running here and there in pursuit of artificial and temporary happiness in temporary power, temporary money, temporary things. Hell is real. Hell is permanent. Hell is dark, bottomless, smelly, hideous, scary, and inescapable. Only the perfect can go to heaven. Since none of us is perfect, we need Jesus who was perfect for us. Crash our way into heaven? Never happen. Fall easily into hell? Please, do not let it happen. Eternity is a long, long, long time, a never-ending time.

# 15. Relationship With God the Father

## OF GOD THE FATHER

*Matthew 10:1, 19-20; Romans 8:14-16; Galatians 4:4-6*

Paul explains that we who are led by the Spirit of God are adopted sons **of God** and call him **Father** (Romans 8:14-16 and Galatians 4:4-6).

Jesus warned his apostles when he appointed them that some day they would be delivered up to governments and Jesus' enemies, but they were not to worry what to say, "for it will be given to you in that hour what you should speak for it is not you who speak, but the Spirit **of your Father** who speaks in you" (Matthew 10:1, 19-20).

We could say that the Father is the Will/Mind part of God. The Father is the decision maker part of God, the First Cause. The Spirit is the life-giving part of God ~ the force that created life on earth, and creates spiritual life in us so that we move into action.

In our physical bodies, what part tells arms and legs what to do? What part of us has to be obeyed by the rest of our body, just like a parent? It is our mind, or will.

It is the same with our spirit which is the life-giver. Our mind/will may decide to invent something. But if our idea is not practical, our idea will not ever see the light of day.

Our mind/will may decide to run in a race and win. Our mind/will puts our motivation in our body to start working out. But, if our mind/will does not motivate our spirit enough, our spirit will not motivate our legs to get out there and practice. If we do not have enough spirit in us to win the race, our mind/will will be disappointed because neither our spirit nor our body obeyed our mind/will.

Each of us is one, even though we may speak proudly of our mind passing that test, our spirit strong enough it made our legs run a mile. Or we may say, "I did not have my mind on that," or "I just didn't have the spirit in me to go on that diet." We may speak of our mind, our body, and our spirit as though they were individual entitles even though we know we are one.

We cannot get anything done that our mind/will decides for us to get done without our spirit motivating us to do it, to carry it out, to make the decision a reality.

## GIVE/SEND/SUPPLY/RECEIVE

*Luke 11:13; John 3:34-35; John 14:26; John 20:20-22; Acts 5:32; Acts 15:3, 8; I Corinthians 2:10-16; II Corinthians 1:21-22; II Corinthians 5:2-5; Galatians 3:5-7; I Thessalonians 4:8; I John 4:13-14*

When someone dies, people say his spirit left his body. Therefore, the natural human spirit within us gives our bodies life. The Holy Spirit does the same thing. God, the Mind, sends his Spirit to our soul to keep us spiritually alive. God, the Mind, also sends his Spirit to our body, so we will put into action things God wants us to do.

When God, the Mind, sends signals to us on how to act, those signals are his Spirit. I Corinthians 2:10-16 explains that the Spirit searches the Mind of God and communicates them to our minds so the Spirit can put those things into action. What is the Mind of God? Those things which were turned into Words. Since the Holy Spirit is the Word of God (John 14:17 and 17:17), when we search the scriptures, the Holy Spirit helps us put God's Mind in our heart. We must know how to act before we actually act. The mind tells the body what to do. (See the illustration in this chapter.)

"We are his witnesses to these things, and so also is the Holy Spirit whom God has **given** to those who obey him" (Acts 5:32).

## SPEECH/TRUTH/WISDOM/PROPHECY

*Matthew 10:1, 19-20; John 14:15-17; John 15:24-27;*

*I Corinthians 7:39-40; I Corinthians 12:3; II Corinthians 3:3; Ephesians 1:13-14, 17, 20; I John 4:1-2; Revelation 19:10*

"Therefore, I make known to you that no one **speaking** by the Spirit of God [the Father] calls Jesus accursed, and no one can **say** that Jesus is Lord except by the Holy Spirit" (I Corinthians 12:3). How do we know Jesus is Lord? By reading his Word. Who is his Word today?

"When the Helper comes whom I shall send to you from the Father, the Spirit of **Truth** who proceeds from the Father, he will testify of me....Your word is **truth** (John 15:26; 17:17). Just because God's words are no longer audible words of the Spirit, it does not mean the written words are not of the Spirit.

"...the God of our Lord Jesus Christ, the Father of glory, may give you of his Spirit of **wisdom** in the knowledge of him" (Ephesians 1:17).

At first, the Truth (God's Word) was spoken and spread around the world by people who could also perform miracles so they could prove their words were from God the Father. Today the miracle is the Bible, for it has survived thousands of years, despite having been trashed, torn, burned, and buried, and with no changes or alterations.

II Corinthians 3:3 says the Word of God is written in our hearts. How did it get there? By putting it in our mind first, then believing it, then putting it in our heart so we will act on it.

## IN/WITH

*Luke 10:21; Acts 1:4-5; Acts 10:38; Romans 2:25, 29; Romans 8:9; Philippians 3:3; Revelation 21:10*

Jesus was **in the** Spirit when he thanked God the Father for giving the words of life to receptive people (Luke 10:21).

The apostle John, now in his old age, and now the only one left of the old group of twelve who followed Jesus around, was **in the** Spirit when he was carried away to a high mountain to see the holy Jerusalem coming down out of heaven from God [the Father] (Revelaion21:10).

When we refuse to live our life according to fleshly desires, but rather according to spiritual desires, we have the Spirit of God [the Father] dwelling **in** us (Romans 8:9; Philippians 3:3).

# OF/FROM

*Matthew 28:19-20; John 3:5-6; Acts 2:32-33; Acts 7:55;*
*Romans 8:27; Romans 15:13; I Corinthians 6:16-20;*
*II Corinthians 13:14; I Peter 1:2*

When God the Father sends his Spirit, how do we receive him? First, we admit we are sinful. Without that admission, we cannot take the first steps to receiving the Spirit.

"He who is joined to the Lord is one spirit with him. Flee sexual immorality....Or do you not know that your body is the temple **of** the Holy Spirit who is in you, whom you have **from** God [the Father] and you are not your own? You were bought at a price; therefore, glorify God in your body and in your spirit which are God's" (I Corinthians 6:17-20).

Then we recognize God the Father's grace and love for us (II Corinthians 13:14), and the sanctification (purification) that can be received **of** the Spirit (I Peter 1:2).

Next, we, according to Jesus' instructions, are baptized "in the name of the Father, and of the Son, and **of** the Holy Spirit" (Matthew 18:19). As a result, we are born **of** the Spirit (John 3:56 ~ Jesus' own words).

Then we have from the Father the promise **of** the Holy Spirit guaranteeing our salvation from hell (Acts 2:32-38). Then we have the mind **of** the Spirit according to the will of God, the Father (Romans 8:27). And that is when our bodies become the temple **of** the Holy Spirit (I Corinthians 6:19-20).

Now that we are the temple of the Holy Spirit, we must take care of it. Do we feed ourselves spiritually every day to keep it alive? Do we feed others spiritually every day to help them keep theirs alive?

# BY/ACCORDING TO

*Matthew 12:28; Romans 5:5; Romans 6:4, 6: 8:3-4; Romans 8:14-16; I Corinthians 6:9-11; Ephesians 3:2, 5; II Thessalonians 2:13; I Peter 3:18; II Peter 1:20-21*

Romans 8:1416 says we are led by the Spirit of God to be sons of God and call him Father. We must, therefore, walk, not according to our fleshly desires and all the fun we could be having, but according to the Spirit, to the glory of the Father (Romans 6:4-6; 8:3-4).

God, the Father/Mind, sends us his Spirit through the neuron transmitters of the Word. Our spirit/body responds by doing what God the Father/Mind through the Word tells us to do. Our actions in responding to the Word is God's Spirit in us.

How much competition does our mind give God's Mind? How much competition does our spirit give God's Spirit? Only when our mind steps aside will the Mind of God be able to take control. Then we will let God's Spirit live in our bodies and move us into action.

God will not force himself on us. He has given us free will. Otherwise, our love and our actions would not be our own. But God pleads with us every day, waiting patiently because he does not want anyone to be lost (II Peter 3:9).

# GOD'S ATTRIBUTES

*Romans 1:2-4; Ephesians 4:30; II Timothy 1:7; Hebrews 2:4; Hebrews 10:29-31; I Peter 4:14*

Romans 1:4 refers to God the Father's Spirit of holiness, not worldliness. II Timothy 1:7 refers to God's Spirit of power, love, and a sound mind, not a mind of fear. Hebrews 10:29 refers to God's Spirit of grace, not vengeance. I Peter 4:14 refers to the Spirit of the glory of God, the Father.

Just what is God the Father's glory? God's glory is all that he is and does. When Moses wanted to see God's glory, God replied that he would make his goodness pass before him (Exodus 33:18-19a). When God descended, he proclaimed he was merciful, gracious, longsuffering, abounding in goodness, abounding in truth, keeping mercy for thousands, forgiving sins, and protecting us by the boomerang effect from sinners who refuse to repent (Exodus 34:5-7).

How do we know we have the Spirit in us? By obeying God's commands. How does the world know we have the Spirit in us? By hearing us teach, and watching us do. We can't just teach any words we want to, and we can't just do anything we want to. They are a duo that must work together.

We can teach when we read the Bible to someone every day, or encourage a child to call us every day to read a Bible verse to us. We can pray for the lost every day, including loved ones, our neighbors, and people in the newspaper.

We can do it by telephoning or emailing someone every morning who lives alone, taking someone's mail or newspaper to their door, sending notes of encouragement, visiting nursing homes, taking an orphan (by death or divorce) out for a coke. My book, *Applied Christianity: A Handbook of 500 Good Works,* is packed full of practical how-to's for every imaginable type of good work.

Dare to eliminate the frivolous and unimportant and make time in your every day to have the mind of the Father in you so his Spirit can lead you to act.

# ETERNAL/ONE/SEVEN

*Matthew 3:16-17; John 4:23-24; Acts 2:17-22; Ephesians 4:4-6;*
*Hebrews 9:14; Revelation 1:4; Revelation 4:5; Revelation 5:6*

How can God be one when people claim there are three Persons? This three Persons phrase was started by the Catholic Church several centuries after Jesus lived on earth. The Bible never says "trinity." God is one God.

Someone asks, "How can God have a Son if the Son was as eternal as God?".

Everyone has thoughts. We create our thoughts, but our thoughts have existed as long as we have. Our words are our thoughts in audible form. Since God has always been able to speak, his thoughts and words have existed as long as he has, even though created by him.

Every person is made up of a mind, spirit, and body. It does not make us three; we are still one. Our spirit keeps us alive and doing, and our mind tells our body and words what to do to communicate with others. So, too, God is made up of mind/will (the Father), Spirit (life, animation, motivation), and a way to communicate with us ~ sometimes in word form and sometimes in body form. Another way God communicates with us is through his Spirit.

All three essences make up the one God, and all three have always existed (Ephesians 4:4-6).

Sometimes in the Bible, the Holy Spirit of God is identified as being seven (Revelation 4:5 and 5:6). Numbers in Revelation are always symbolic. Three represents the three parts of God in heaven. Four represents the earth ~ four winds, four corners of the earth, etc. Therefore, whenever God's Spirit is said to be seven, it indicates that God is everywhere ~ both in heaven and on earth.

# 16. Relationship with God the Son

## WHO WAS JESUS
## In Bible Times?

Jesus was the Word of God in flesh. He was the Word of God we could watch and listen to (John 1:1, 14). He used his physical activities as proof of who he was by fulfilling all the prophecies about him made centuries earlier and by performing miracles (John 20:30-31).

Jesus was at the creation of the world. The Mind/Will of God the Father decided to make the world. The Spirit of God hovered over it to turn it into reality. The Word/Son of God spoke all things into existence. "In the beginning was the Word, and the Word was with God, and the Word was God. He was in the beginning with God. All things were made through him, and without him nothing was made that was made" (John1:1-3,14,18).

God's Spirit has appeared in physically in only two forms. John 1:32-33 says he descended like a dove. Did he forever remain in the form of a dove? No. Later, he came in the form of tongues of fire (Acts 2:3-4). Did he remain forever in the form of fire? No. Therefore, even though Jesus appeared for a while in the form of a human, it doesn't necessarily mean he kept that same form. Jesus was the seeable and audible manifestation of God on earth. He was God materialized.

When Adam and Eve walked with God in the cool of the evening (Genesis 3:8), that was Jesus.

When the Angel of the Lord appeared to Hagar (Genesis 16:7-13), that was Jesus.

When the Lord appeared to Abraham in the form of three men (Genesis 18:1-33), that was Jesus.

When the Angel of the Lord stopped Abraham from

sacrificing Isaac (Genesis 22:11-16), that was Jesus.

When God appeared to Moses in a burning bush (Exodus 3:1-6), that was Jesus.

When the Angel of the Lord led the Israelites through the wilderness in the pillar (Exodus 23:20-22), that was Jesus.

When the rock poured forth water for the Israelites in the wilderness, that was Jesus (I Corinthians 10:1-4).

When the Angel of the Lord stood with his sword drawn in the road to block Balaam (Numbers 22:22-35), that was Jesus.

When the Angel of the Lord appeared as a man with his sword drawn to Joshua (Joshua 5:13-15), that was Jesus.

When the Angel of the Lord appeared to all the Israelites and told them he had led them through the wilderness, and gave them instructions about the Promised Land (Judges 1:1-4), that was Jesus.

When the Angel of the Lord appeared to Gideon and performed some miracles (Judges 6:11-23), that was Jesus.

When the Angel of the Lord appeared to Samson's parents to tell them of their baby, Samson, (Judges 13), that was Jesus.

When the Son of God walked around the furnace of fire with Shadrach, Meshach, and Abednego (Daniel 3:16-25), that was Jesus.

John 1:14 says the "Word became flesh and dwelt among us, and we beheld his glory, the glory as of the only-begotten of the Father, full of grace and truth." I Timothy 3:16 says "God was manifested in the flesh, justified in the Spirit, seen by angels, preached among the Gentiles, believed on in the world, and received up in glory."

John 1:18 says no one has seen God at any time. Why is that? It is impossible for us to see God. God is larger than everything he created. Scientists tell us there are two trillion galaxies out there. Further, every galaxy has one hundred thousand billion stars. God is larger than that; therefore, it is impossible to see God.

But his only begotten Son declared him. The Father/Mind/Will decided to put his Words in physical and audible form because he put us in a physical and audible world at the creation. And in John 14:9b, Jesus said whoever had seen Jesus had seen the Father.

Why did Jesus become flesh when he was born to Mary, and stay awhile on earth? Hebrews 10 explains that God prepared a body for him so he could spill his blood and become a sacrifice to die both physically and spiritually for us on the cross.

Now in heaven, he sometimes takes on the recognizable form he had while on earth as he did for Stephen just prior to his death (Acts 7:55), and sometimes he takes on the form of a bloody lamb (Revelation 5:6).

AFTER JESUS RETURNED TO HEAVEN, HE HANDED OVER
HIS FUNCTION AS THE WORD IN SEEABLE AND AUDIBLE
FORM TO THE SPIRIT AS THE WORD
IN AUDIBLE, THEN READABLE FORM.

# WHO IS JESUS
## In Modern Times?

Jesus said in John 14:16-18 that he had to return to heaven so he could send another helper, the Spirit of Truth. Jesus had already called himself the truth (John 14:6). So, why did he have to go? He explained it in John 14:18 when he said: "I will not leave you orphans; I will come to you." Jesus had to take his human body away, the body that could only be seen and heard from a few feet away, so he could be with all Christians everywhere all at the same time.

After that, instead of preaching sermons and giving advice, Jesus motivates us through his Spirit.

The Spirit of Jesus would not let Paul go into the northern province of Bithynia, so he went to the seaport of Troas where he had a vision to go over to Macedonia (Acts 16:7). Paul said he would be delivered from prison because of the prayers and help of the Spirit of Jesus Christ (Philippians 1:18-21).

Hebrews 7:25 says Jesus is our intercessor. Romans 8:26-27 says the Holy Spirit is our intercessor. Both were and are the Word.

After Jesus returned to heaven, the Spirit took over being the Word. Jesus was the audible and seeable Word, then the Holy Spirit became the temporary audible Word during the days of the Apostles, and finally the permanent written Word once the Bible was written.

## GIVE/SEND/LEAD/SUPPLY/RECEIVE

*Matthew 12:15-21; Luke 1:35; John 1:32-34; John 3:34-35;*
*John 7:38-39; John 14:16-18; John 20:20-22; Acts 8:16-17;*
*Acts 19:2-7; Romans 8:14-15; Ephesians 1:17; I John 3:23-24;*
*Revelation 5:6*

While on earth, God had the Spirit in him fully and completely. "For he whom God has sent speaks the words of God, for God [the Father] does not **give** the Spirit by measure" (John 3:34-35).

For the rest of us, Jesus said in John 3:8 that, at baptism of water and the Spirit, we are born again to a new life. "Repent, and let every one of you be baptized in the name of Jesus Christ for the remission of sins; and you shall **receive** the gift of the Holy Spirit" (Acts 2:38). "Therefore, we were buried with him through baptism into death, that just as Christ was raised from the dead by the glory of the Father, even so we also should walk in newness of life" (Romans 6:4).

Then, all who are **led** by the Spirit of God (motivated, given life) are considered sons of God, adopted (Romans 8:14-15) to do what Jesus did ~ go about seeking and saving the lost (Luke 9:10). The beatitude says when we make peace between man and God, we are sons of God (Matthew 5:9).

## OF/FROM

*Matthew 3:16-17; John 14:16-18; Romans 1:2-4; Romans 8:11;*
*Ephesians 1:17; I John 4:1-2; Revelation 1:4-5; Revelation 19:10*

After Jesus' baptism and subsequent temptations on how to get the kingdom of God started Satan's way, Jesus returned in the power **of the** Spirit (Luke 4:14). He now had miraculous powers (see the study of power in a previous chapter). Remember, the Spirit is always the one who makes things happen; and in this case, it was to prove Jesus' words were the Word of God. Over and over we see the intermingling of power and the Word.

At the end of his ministry, Jesus told his apostles to go and "make disciples of all nations, baptizing them in the name of the Father and of the Son and **of the** Holy Spirit, teaching them to observe all things I have commanded you; and lo, I am with you always, even to the end of the age" (Matthew 28:19-20).

Paul, while in prison, said, "I know that this will turn out for my deliverance through your prayer and the supply **of the** Spirit of Jesus Christ" (Philippians 1:19).

Jesus always had the Spirit, and sometimes Jesus was the Spirit. Remember, God the Father is the Mind. God the Son is the physical transmission of God's Mind in words (like nerves in our body), and the Holy Spirit is our body's response to those words.

## BY/THROUGH/WITH

*Matthew 4:1; Luke 4:1-2; John 1:32-33; Acts 1:1-2; Acts 10:38; Acts 13:2-4; Romans 8:11; Romans 8:14-15; Romans 15:16; I Corinthians 6:11; I Corinthians 12:3; Ephesians 2:13, 18; Ephesians 3:4-6; I John 3:23-24*

After Jesus' baptism when the Spirit descended on him (John 1:32-33), he was led up **by** the Spirit into the wilderness to be tempted by the devil (Matthew 4:1). He needed to think through things on how to begin his kingdom.

I do not believe he was having a conversation with Jesus sitting on one rock and Satan sitting on another rock. I believe Satan was in Jesus' head tempting him. Jesus had to have time to sort through things. God's Spirit in us makes us conscious of decisions to be made, and sometimes they need to be done in private, weighing the pros and cons.

It took Jesus over a month to work through them. His knowledge of the Bible (his own words) got him through it. Interestingly, his answers were from Deuteronomy where Moses recalled to the people their journey through the wilderness as they prepared to set up their new kingdom in the Promised Land. Jesus stayed in his wilderness until he was convinced of the way to introduce the kingdom to the world. When he came out of that wilderness, he had the power of miracles **by** the power of the Holy Spirit (Acts 10:38).

Later, Jesus was raised from death **through** the Holy Spirit (Romans 8:11).

## OF THE

*Matthew 1:18, 20; Matthew 28:19-20; Luke 4:14; Luke 4:14; Luke 4:16-18; Luke 9:54-56; Acts 2:3233; Acts 8:39-40; Romans 8:1-2; Romans 15:30; II Corinthians 13:14; Galatians 3:14; Philippians 1:18-21; I Peter 1:2*

Jesus was conceived in Mary by the power **of** the Holy Spirit (Matthew 1:18, 20). When he began his ministry in Galilee, he had the miraculous power of the Spirit (Luke 4:14. He announced that he was the one predicted to have the Spirit **of** the Lord upon him and to have been anointed to preach the gospel and proclaim liberty (Luke 4:16-18)

After Jesus returned to heaven, his Holy Spirit is poured out onto us (Acts 2:32-33). Today, the Spirit sanctifies us because of our obedience and Jesus having shed his blood for us (I Peter 1:2).

## IN

*Mark 2:8; Luke 10:21; Galatians 3:1-3; Ephesians 2:21-22; Philippians 3:3*

Jesus used the Spirit **in** him to perceive what people around him were thinking (Mark 2:8). He rejoiced **in** the Spirit, thanking the Father for revealing the wisdom and salvation of God to innocent people rather than world leaders (Luke 10:21).

Today, we worship God **in** Spirit and in Christ Jesus (Philippians 3:3), for the Spirit Jesus sent to us after he returned to heaven was himself (John 14:16-18). Jesus, the Word of God, often is interchangeable with the Spirit, also the Word of God.

# SPEAK/SAY

*Matthew 8:16; Matthew 12:31-32; Acts 13:2-4; I Corinthians 12:3;
I John 5:6-8; Revelation 22:16-17*

Jesus used the miraculous powers of the Holy Spirit to prove his Words were the Words of God from the Mind of God (John 20:30-31). Later the Spirit urged the Christians into action. In Acts 13:2-4, after fasting, the Holy Spirit **said** to the Christians in Antioch to send Barnabas and Saul/Paul to spread the gospel of Jesus. Then, they were sent out by the Holy Spirit to Cyprus and elsewhere (Acts 13:2-4).

The Holy Spirit has a great marketing plan, a great advertising campaign for the church. It isn't just worship, though that is the highlight of what we do on Sundays. But it is also speaking of the Word of God and what Jesus did for us with others so they, too, can be saved (I Corinthians 12:3).

# PRESENT

The Word of God ~ the story of Jesus and his conquering death for us ~ lives on today by miraculous preservation. The Bible, the Word of God, has survived every possible attack, but it lives on. It goes all the way back to the beginning of time. No other book in existence does that. It survives because of the actions of the Holy Spirit to preserve his Words through courageous men and women down through the centuries. (For more on the survival of the Bible, go to my book, *Worship, the First-Century Way*.)

The church of God, the body of Christ, the temple of the Spirit, lives on today by miraculous preservation. Brave men and women laid down their lives rather than change the way the church was set up by Jesus and his apostles so long ago. It has survived every attempt at extinction because the Holy Spirit taught and urged Christians everywhere to preserve the church, and do so with their lives if need be. (For more on the survival of the church, go to my book, *Worship Changes Since the First Century*.)

## FUTURE

I Thessalonians 4:16-17 says that someday Jesus will descend from heaven and the dead in Christ will rise first. Then Christians who are alive will join them in the air where we will ever be with the Lord (not on earth, but in heaven).

Then will come the judgment and everyone will make two confessions. First, they will give an account of themselves to God (Romans 14:11-12), and everyone will bow to Jesus and confess that he is truly the Lord to the glory of God the Father.

Jesus said, "Behold, I am coming soon! My reward is with me....I am the Alpha and the Omega, the First and the Last, the Beginning and the end. Blessed are those who wash their robes, that they may have the right to the tree of life and may go through the gates into the city. Outside are the dogs, those who practice magic arts, the sexually immoral, the murderers, the idolaters and everyone who loves and practices falsehood [lies]."

Until then, the Spirit remains with us on earth with the Bride of Christ, the church. Revelation 22:17 and 20 say the church and the Spirit within us cry out daily, "Come, Lord Jesus!" And Jesus replies, "Yes, I am coming soon!"

And until then, we cling to the Word of God, the Spirit of God, who teaches us and quickens us and puts us into action to be Christ's ambassadors on earth. Until the end of time.

*For more on Jesus' relationship with his Will (the Father) and his*

107

*Spirit (motivator and animator) read my book, WAS JESUS GOD? available at any bookseller.*

# Thank You

Thanks for reading my book! I'm so honored that you chose to spend your precious time with my research. You are appreciated. I'm an independent author who relies on my readers to help spread the word about stories you enjoy. Would you take a few minutes to let your friends know on Facebook, Pinterest... wherever you spend your time online?

Also, each honest review at online retailers means a lot to me and helps other readers know if this is a book they might enjoy,

I welcome contact from readers. At my website (below), you can do so. You can also sign up for my newsletter (below) to be notified of half-price books and new releases.

# BUY YOUR NEXT BOOK NOW
## CHRISTIAN LIFE
Applied Christianity: Handbook 500 Good Works
You Can Be a Hero Alone
Worship Changes Since 1st Century + Worship 1sr Century Way
The Best of Alexander Campbell's Millennial Harbinger
Inside the Hearts of Bible Women-Reader+Audio+Leader
The Lord's Supper: 52 Readings with Prayers
http://bit.ly/Christianlife

## BIBLE TEXT STUDIES
Revelation: A Love Letter From God
The Holy Spirit: 592 Verses Examined
Was Jesus God? (Why Evil)
365 Life-Changing Scriptures Day by Date
Love Letters of Jesus & His Bride, Ecclesia
Christianity or Islam? The Contrast
The Road to Heaven
http://bit.ly/BibleTexts

## FUN BOOKS
Bible Puzzles, Bible Song Book, Bible Numbers
http://bit.ly/BibleFun

## TOUCHING GOD SERIES
365 Golden Bible Thoughts: God's Heart to Yours
365 Pearls of Wisdom: God's Soul to Yours
365 Silver-Winged Prayers: Your Spirit to God's
http://bit.ly/TouchingGodSeries

## -SURVEY SERIES: EASY BIBLE WORKBOOKS
→Old Testament & New Testament Surveys
→Questions You Have Asked-Part I & II
http://bit.ly/BibleWorkbooks

## HISTORICAL RESEARCH BIBLE
for Novel, Screenwriter, Documentary & Thesis Writers
http://bit.ly/32uZkHa

## GENEALOGY: How to Climb Your Family Tree Without Falling Out
Volume I & 2: Beginner-Intermediate & Colonial-Medieval
http://bit.ly/GenealogyBeginner-Advanced

# About the Author

Katheryn Maddox Haddad grew up in the cold north and now lives in Arizona where she does not have to shovel sunshine. She basks in 100-degree weather with palm trees, cacti, and a computer with most of the lettering worn off.

She has a bachelor's degree in English, Bible, and history, from Harding University, a Master's Degree in management and human relations from Abilene Christian University, and part of a Master's Degree in Bible from Harding University, including Greek studies.

She spends half her day writing, and the other half teaching English over the internet worldwide using the Bible as textbook through World English Institute. She has taught some 7000 Muslims, mostly in the Middle East. Students she has converted to Christianity are in hiding in Afghanistan, Iran, Iraq, Yemen, Jordan, Somalia, Sierra Leone, Uzbekistan, Tajikistan, Indonesia, and Palestine. "They are my heroes," she says.

In addition to her seventy-seven books (non-fiction, novels, and storybooks), she has written numerous articles for *Gospel Advocate, Twentieth Century Christian, Firm Foundation, Christian Bible Teacher, Christian Woman,* and several world mission publications. Her weekly column, *Little-Known Facts About the Bible,* appeared several years in newspapers in North Carolina and Texas.

# CONNECT WITH THE AUTHOR

Website: **https://inspirationsbykatheryn.com**

Facebook: **bit.ly/FacebooksKatherynMaddoxHaddad**

Linkedin: **http://bit.ly/KatherynLinkedin**

Twitter: **https://twitter.com/KatherynHaddad**

Pinterest: **https://www.pinterest.com/haddad1940/**

Goodreads:
**https://www.goodreads.com/katherynmaddoxhaddad**

## Get A Free Book
Sign up for Katheryn's monthly newsletter with half-price books
for the whole family and insider tips on what's coming next.
**http://bit.ly/katheryn**

## Join My Dream Team
Members get the first peek at my newest book and have fun
offering me advice sometimes. I have a point system of rewards
for helping me get the word out. Check it out here:
**http://bit.ly/KatherynsDreamTeam**

# ALL VERSES WITH "SPIRIT"

## It's Your Turn

Beginning the next page are all the scriptures in the Bible referring to God's Holy Spirit, also sometimes called Jesus' Holy Spirit.

Perhaps you would like to create your own study of the Holy Spirit. Remember, stay faithful to the scriptures, not your opinions. God's Word is the only Truth.

# OLD TESTAMENT

Genesis 1:1-2
Genesis 6:3-6
Genesis 41:38-39

Exodus 28:3
Exodus 31:3
Exodus 35:30-31

Numbers 11:16-17
Numbers 11:25
Numbers 11:26-28
Numbers 16:19
Numbers 24:1-2, 13-14
Numbers 27:16-18

Deuteronomy 34:9

Judges 3:9-10
Judges 6:34-36
Judges 11:1, 29
Judges 13:2
Judges 14:6
Judges 14:19
Judges 15:14-15

I Samuel 10:1, 5-10
I Samuel 11:1, 6
I Samuel 16:13
I Samuel 16:14
I Samuel 16:15
I Samuel 16:16, 23
I Samuel 18:9-12
I Samuel 19:9-10
I Samuel 19:18-20
I Samuel 19:23-24

II Samuel 23:1-2

I Kings 18:12

II Kings 2:9-10
II Kings 2:15
II Kings 2:16

I Chronicles 12:14, 18
I Chronicles 28:11-12

II Chronicles 15:1-3
II Chronicles 20:14-15
II Chronicles 24:20-24

Nehemiah 9:19-21
Nehemiah 9:30

Job 26:13
Job 27:3
Job 32:7-8
Job 33:4
Job 34:14-15

Psalm 51:10-17
Psalm 104:30
Psalm 106:33
Psalm 139:7
Psalm 143:4, 7, 10

Proverbs 1:20, 23

Ecclesiastes 12:7

Isaiah 4:4
Isaiah 11:1-2
Isaiah 28:6
Isaiah 30:1
Isaiah 32:15-16
Isaiah 34:16

Isaiah 40:7-8
Isaiah 40:13-14
Isaiah 42:1
Isaiah 42:5
Isaiah 44:3
Isaiah 48:16
Isaiah 59:19-20
Isaiah 59:21
Isaiah 61:1
Isaiah 63:10
Isaiah 63:11-14

Ezekiel 2:2-3
Ezekiel 3:12
Ezekiel 4:14-15
Ezekiel 3:24-25
Ezekiel 8:2-3
Ezekiel 11:1-2
Ezekiel 11:5
Ezekiel 11:19f
Ezekiel 11:24
Ezekiel 18:31
Ezekiel 36:26-27
Ezekiel 37:14
Ezekiel 39:29
Ezekiel 43:5

Hosea 9:7

Joel 2:28-29

Micah 2:7
Micah 3:8

Haggai 1:14
Haggai 2:5-6

Zechariah 4:6
Zechariah 6:5, 8

Zechariah 7:12
Zechariah 12:10

# NEW TESTAMENT

Matthew 1:18,20
Matthew 3:11
Matthew 3:16
Matthew 4:1
Matthew 4:23
Matthew 8:5, 13
Matthew 8:16
Matthew 9:18, 25
Matthew 9:35
Matthew 10:1, 19-20
Matthew 12:15
Matthew 12:18, 21
Matthew 12:28
Matthew 12:31-32
Matthew 22:43
Matthew 28:19-20

Mark 1:8
Mark 1:10
Mark 1:12
Mark 2:8
Mark 3:29
Mark 12:36
Mark 13:11
Mark 14:38
Mark 16:17-18

Luke 1:15, 41
Luke 1:35
Luke 1:67
Luke 2:25-27
Luke 3:16
Luke 3:22
Luke 4:1

115

Luke 4:14
Luke 4:16-18
Luke 7:12, 15
Luke 9:54-55
Luke 10:21
Luke 11:13
Luke 12:10-12

John 3:5-6
John 3:7-8
John 3:34-35
John 4:23-24
John 6:63
John 7:38-39
John 11:33
John 11:39, 44
John 13:21
John 14:15-16
John 14:17
John 14:18
John 14:20-21
John 14:26
John 15:24-27
John 16:7
John 16:8
John 20:20-22

Acts 1:1-2
Acts 1:4-5
Acts 1:8
Acts 1:16
Acts 2:1-4
Acts 2:6-7, 14
Acts 2:17a
Acts 2:17b
Acts 2:17c
Acts 2:18
Acts 2:19a
Acts 2:19b

Acts 2:19c
Acts 2:20a
Acts 2:20b
Acts 2:22
Acts 2:32-33
Acts 2:38
Acts 2:43
Acts 4:5-8
Acts 4:23, 31
Acts 4:30
Acts 5:1-5
Acts 5:8-9
Acts 5:12
Acts 5:16
Acts 5:32
Acts 6:3-5
Acts 6:10
Acts 7:51
Acts 7:55
Acts 8:14-19
Acts 8:18
Acts 8:28-29
Acts 8:39-40
Acts 9:10, 17-19
Acts 9:31
Acts 9:33-35
Acts 9:40
Acts 10:19-20
Acts 10:38
Acts 10:44-46
Acts 10:47
Acts 11:12
Acts 11:15
Acts 11:16
Acts 11:22-24
Acts 11:28
Acts 13:2-4
Acts 13:8-10
Acts 13:49-52

Acts 14:8-10
Acts 14:3
Acts 15:3, 8
Acts 16:6-7
Acts 19:2-7
Acts 20:17, 28
Acts 20:22
Acts 20:23
Acts 20:17, 28
Acts 21:4, 10-12
Acts 23:9
Acts 28:5
Acts 28:17, 25-26

Romans 1:2-4
Romans 1:11
Romans 2:25, 29
Romans 5:5
Romans 6:4, 6
Romans 7:6
Romans 7:13-15
Romans 8:1-2
Romans 8:3-4
Romans 8:5
Romans 8:6-7
Romans 8:9
Romans 8:11
Romans 8:13
Romans 8:14-15
Romans 8:16
Romans 8:23
Romans 8:26
Romans 8:27
Romans 9:1
Romans 12:6-8
Romans 14:17-18
Romans 15:13
Romans 15:16
Romans 15:18-19

Romans 15:26-28
Romans 15:30

I Corinthians 1:6-7
I Corinthians 2:4
I Corinthians 2:10-11
I Corinthians 2:12
I Corinthians 2:14-15
I Corinthians 3:16-17
I Corinthians 6:9-11
I Corinthians 6:16-18
I Corinthians 7:39-40
I Corinthians 9:11, 18
I Corinthians 10:3-5
I Corinthians 12:1
I Corinthians 12:3
I Corinthians 12:4-5
I Corinthians 12:7
I Corinthians 12:8
I Corinthians 12:9
I Corinthians 12:10
I Corinthians 12:11
I Corinthians 12:13
I Corinthians 13:8
I Corinthians 14:1
I Corinthians 14:37
I Corinthians 15:42-46

II Corinthians 1:22
II Corinthians 3:3
II Corinthians 3:6
II Corinthians 3:7-8
II Corinthians 3:16-18
II Corinthians 5:2-4
II Corinthians 6:6
II Corinthians 12:1-2
II Corinthians 12:12
II Corinthians 13:14

Galatians 3:1-2
Galatians 3:3
Galatians 3:5
Galatians 3:14
Galatians 4:4-6
Galatians 4:29
Galatians 5:5-6
Galatians 5:16
Galatians 5:17-18
Galatians 5:22
Galatians 6:1
Galatians 6:78

Ephesians 1:3, 5
Ephesians 1:13
Ephesians 1:17
Ephesians 2:13, 18
Ephesians 2:21-22
Ephesians 3:4-6
Ephesians 3:16
Ephesians 4:3
Ephesians 4:4-6
Ephesians 4:30
Ephesians 5:18-19
Ephesians 6:12
Ephesians 6:17
Ephesians 6:18

Philippians 1:17-21
Philippians 2:1
Philippians 3:3

Colossians 1:8
Colossians 1:9
Colossians 3:16

I Thessalonians 1:5
I Thessalonians 1:6
I Thessalonians 4:8

II Thessalonians 2:8-9
II Thessalonians 2:13

I Timothy 3:16
I Timothy 4:1-2

II Timothy 1:7
II Timothy 1:14

Titus 3:5

Hebrews 2:4
Hebrews 3:7
Hebrews 4:12-13
Hebrews 6:4
Hebrews 9:8
Hebrews 9:14
Hebrews 10:15
Hebrews 10:26-28

I Peter 1:2
I Peter 1:10-11
I Peter 1:12
I Peter 3:4, 7
I Peter 3:18
I Peter 4:14

II Peter 1:21
II Peter 2:5

I John 3:24
I John 4:1-2
I John 4:6
I John 4:13-14
I John 5:6-8

Jude 1:15-19
Jude 1:20

Revelation 1:4
Revelation 1:10
Revelation 2:7, 11, 17, 29
Revelation 3:1
Revelation 4:2
Revelation 4:5
Revelation 5:6
Revelation 14:13
Revelation 17:3
Revelation 19:10
Revelation 21:10
Revelation 22:17

www.ingramcontent.com/pod-product-compliance
Lightning Source LLC
Chambersburg PA
CBHW071234020426
42333CB00015B/1467